P9-CKE-146

LARNER, Jeremy. Nobody knows; reflections on the McCarthy campaign of 1968. Macmillan, 1970. 189p 70-95181. 4.95

Unfortunately, *Nobody knows* is politically and psychologically shallow; it seems primarily an ego trip for Larner. The article in *Harper's* in 1969 on which the book is based would be sufficient for any library.

CHOICE *JUNE '71*

Political Science

JEREMY LARNER is primarily a novelist, and has won the Delta Prize and the Aga Khan Prize for his fiction. In addition to his novels, *Drive, He Said* and *The Answer,* he is coauthor of *The Addict in the Street* and *Poverty: Views from the Left.* His stories, essays, and reporting have appeared in *Harper's, Life, Dissent, Paris Review, Partisan Review,* and *The Atlantic Monthly.*

Photograph by Lynne G

"For I believe, based on what I saw as one of his speechwriters from March to September, Wisconsin to Chicago, that McCarthy might have been President. Failing that, he might have given unity and direction to the major forces for progressive change in American life and government. He might have reached out to persuade millions of Americans who remained untouched by the issues which gave rise to his campaign. If I am right in this, his supporters need not talk about America failing them. There is a sense in which the McCarthy campaign failed America, and all who were part of it deserve a chance to think why."—JEREMY LARNER

ALSO BY JEREMY LARNER

Drive, He Said
The Answer
The Addict in the Street *(with Ralph Tefferteller)*
Poverty: Views from the Left *(with Irving Howe)*

NOBODY KNOWS

NOBODY KNOWS

Reflections on the McCarthy Campaign of 1968

☆

BY JEREMY LARNER

The Macmillan Company

Library of Congress Catalog Card Number: 70-95181

FIRST PRINTING

The Macmillan Company
866 Third Avenue, New York, N.Y. 10022
Collier-Macmillan Canada Ltd., Toronto, Ontario

Portions of this book were first published in *Harper's Magazine* in 1969.

Printed in the United States of America

Preface

As one of Senator McCarthy's two speechwriters during most of his 1968 Presidential campaign, working closely with him on a daily basis, I was privy to knowledge from which reporters were excluded, and it was understood that I would keep what I knew to myself. Yet I felt that I was working also for the campaign as a whole, that I was representing many of the others who worked for McCarthy, and that I owed as well a debt to the millions of people who supported us. It seemed to me, finally, after much worry, that my first obligation was to try to explain what happened. The McCarthy campaign was just too important to be mythologized.

Unavoidably, I give some personal description of Senator McCarthy. This is necessary because McCarthy's personality was central to all that happened and all that failed to happen. I do not tell all, as the expression goes, I tell only what I think relevant to the political concerns of the campaign.

Nor do I pretend here to give a full historical account of the campaign. That would be impossible not merely because of my personal involvement, but because all of us are still too close to the events of 1968 to comprehend their connection with the past or their portents for the future. One of the most awesome experiences for me during the campaign was the daily sense of contact with forces that moved beyond our thoughts and purposes. The mosaic form is a confession of fragmentation, as well as an effort to capture how that fragmentation pressed upon us from day to day.

Early in the book I present some partial conclusions about Senator McCarthy's personal qualities. When portions of an earlier version first appeared in *Harper's Magazine*, a few readers accused me of starting with a "personality theory" about McCarthy, then selecting only those events which would back it up. Actually I give my conclusions about McCarthy's personality right up front because I want the reader to see where I am going and not be led by me. But I am not working from theory—my conclusions were the product of day-to-day contact over a six-month campaign, the accumulation of painful experience which I go on to describe in detail.

My concerns here are with the gap between McCarthy and his movement—and, correspondingly, with problems of politics and personality, intentions and achievement, appearance and reality. In pursuing these themes I had to question my own involvement and my own point of view, which I hope I do not conceal or retrospectively refine. I remain unsure about all too many of the subjects I raise, especially those involving the abstraction of "America"—a word which politicians and speechwriters always use with confidence.

Then, too, it should be obvious that I can't pretend to be equally informative about the different parts of the campaign. Naturally I saw much more of the candidate and what happened around him than I did of the larger political operation.

I emphatically do not claim that this book is in any way

the final word on the subject. My original intention was to publish it quickly in a small paperback, so that all those who worked for McCarthy in the summer of '68 might pick up a copy in the summer of '69 and learn more exactly just what they were involved in. I wanted to get to them before they were imposed upon by the Official Versions. But the powers-that-be in the publishing world ruled that McCarthy would be "dead" by the summer of '69 and not worth mass-market distribution. I am obliged, therefore, to inter my little memorial within hard covers.

My reflections in their present form are about 60 percent longer than the material which appeared in *Harper's*. I have been able to restore some anecdotal sections left out of *Harper's* because of space limitations. Also the text itself is quite different. After the *Harper's* articles appeared, I was contacted by hundreds of people who had worked in the campaign, from volunteers in the storefronts to leaders in high national positions. As a result I have been able to add more information—for example, on McCarthy's earlier career. Many of my descriptions have been shaded by complications I was not previously aware of. While my conclusions remain in about the same balance, there is more they must account for.

One picture, I think, has emerged more strongly with the passage of time: that of McCarthy as a personally unusual but conventional politician, suddenly raised on high by a movement that was at once a vindication and an embarrassment.

I have tried, at last, to stick pretty close to what I saw and heard. I have left out a number of interesting occurrences because I could not be sure what I would have thought had I witnessed them myself. The reader can be sure that the firsthand descriptions really are firsthand, and that the others come from extremely reliable sources.

I have many to thank, beginning with Marty and Ann Peretz, who asked me to meet McCarthy and who are not responsible for anything that has happened since.

I must thank Alan Rinzler for first suggesting this book, Willie Morris of *Harper's* for his support and enthusiasm, and Midge Decter and William Bradley for their valuable editorial advice.

I owe thanks to many from the campaign who encouraged me as I worked and offered friendly criticism. Some are in positions where they would rather not be thanked by name. I am most deeply grateful to Steve Cohen, Sy Hersh and Harold Ickes, without whose friendship and help I might not have persevered.

One has to thank Gene McCarthy when all is said and done, though what follows must necessarily be a strange sort of thanks. Without him, none of the events which prompted this book would have taken place. Without him, we would have done much less; indeed, we would not have known what we could do.

We were lucky also to have Jane Taffinder, who came over from England to type nearly every one of Senator McCarthy's speeches and statements in the campaign of '68, including those that stemmed from yours truly.

Finally, this book is for all those who worked to change America in 1968.

May we have another chance.

JEREMY LARNER
June, 1969

NOBODY KNOWS

". . . what my intentions were . . . I think I knew better than some of the people who are telling what they were. And if I'm not saying what they were, why nobody knows."

—from an interview with Senator Eugene J. McCarthy, *Boston Globe*, December 15, 1968

1 His announcement on November 30, 1967, had none of the punchiness of the contemporary press release. He was "concerned" that the Administration had set no "limits" on the price it would pay for victory in Vietnam. He was hopeful that his "challenge" might "alleviate the sense of political helplessness and restore . . . a belief in the processes of American politics."

Eugene McCarthy did not say he was running for President. He was challenging not the President, but "the President's position."

People used to say then that he lacked personality. Those who were tuned in to him knew better almost right away. For us, it was the great big people who lacked true personality. We suspected they had sunk us deeper and deeper in Vietnam for want of real stuff on the inside. They were hollowed out, those high and empty holy ones, they spoke in empty bombast, acted from panic and make-believe, tried to cover up the horror of their deeds with giant masks of super-gravity.

If McCarthy came on flat and careful, it might just be because he tried to say only what he knew. Where other politicians worked to make themselves an "image," to see themselves as others saw them, McCarthy seemed to cherish a private sensibility, to struggle with a refined and exacting conscience. If he made fun of "charisma," refused casting in the star system of American life and thought, why, that was a signal that he possessed a self worthy of the name, that, alone and inside, without anyone's scorecard or fan mag, the man had a genuine existence. If he did not set great store by the horns and drums, perhaps we had found a man who would not lose his head when the horns began to play. Perhaps we had found a leader who could really stand for something.

Those of us who thought we understood him before New Hampshire felt that we were necessarily few in number. Which was a pity, but he didn't have a chance anyhow—did he? America seemed politically impenetrable, controlled at the top by an elite of policy makers who duped and pacified the general population. No wonder only one Senator dared offer himself against the war! If he irritated press and politicians, well, what could one expect? Having suffered too long with false heroes, we gave our anti-hero the benefit of the doubt, and credit for all the ironic virtues each one reserved in secret for himself.

By the end of the year we learned we were righter than we thought—and we were wrong. Clearly McCarthy was not to be pitied or admired for a deficiency of personality. We found he was ready to make his personality the center of his campaign, and to let the cause for which he stood win or lose on the strength of it. Try as we might, his statements and actions could not be wholly understood in terms of his political commitments or his positions on the issues. Again and again, his conduct referred us back to the man's conception of himself; and by the end of the campaign, friends and foes alike were deep in the daily exegesis of his moods and gestures. McCarthy had turned out to be anything but the messenger who humbly effaces himself for the sake of his message, the modest warrior who stands or falls on the virtue of his cause.

His "challenge" may have begun as a test of the issues; but the candidate's stress on his own inner mysteries was so strong and so persistent that the McCarthy campaign became in the end a study of the relation between politics and personality—or if you will, a study of history and the anti-hero.

We learned that McCarthy stood for something, all right. But what he stood for was public and political only by circumstance. Again and again he pointed upward, and we peered through our poor astrolabes to get a sightline. Did we see his star or didn't we? In its loftiness it looked unreal—as distant and as solemn as an image.

2 IN THE FALL OF 1967, THE MOOD OF AMERICANS WHO openly opposed the war was desperate and gloomy. There were respectable liberals who seriously discussed the possibility of "guerrilla action" within the United States. If they read *The Wall Street Journal,* they might have noted that the business community was beginning to realize the war was uneconomic as well as controversial. And there were silent folks, many of them, for whom the war was peculiar and unpleasant, though they did not like people who "spoke against

the country." On television each night as they ate their supper, the American public could view the gap between Vietnam as it was and as our leaders said it was, but it was assumed, even by antiwar columnists and commentators, that a majority of that public did not notice or care.

It was typical enough that after the March on the Pentagon met with public antagonism—for reasons which had little to do with the war itself—those who sympathized with its purpose could readily accept Norman Mailer's metaphysical theory that Vietnam embodied the secret will of "small-town America"—an insatiable lust for annihilation.

Practically no one would have predicted at that point that a reformist political movement which sent student protesters into precisely the heart of small-town America could actually topple the man who was despised as the king of everything small-town, and irreparably shake the public faith in the instincts of our military and the justice of American interventionism.

Yet Allard Lowenstein and a group of student leaders announced just that goal at the conference of the National Student Association in August of 1967. In retrospect, it was an act of faith—a challenge that had to be accepted if they were to keep on telling young people that democratic political action could change America. How could they claim to be the next generation of liberal leaders if they could not lead a popular opposition to the war?

Up till then, Lowenstein had been getting up antiwar petitions—from Rhodes scholars, Peace Corps veterans, student editors, etc.—moving at a frantic pace and frequently leaving others to finish what he began. He had been trying to develop a liberal rhetoric against the war and a democratic form of action which would pull the middle body of American opinion in his direction, rather than repel it, as many of the peace demonstrations up till then had done. Now Lowenstein with his sincerity and his passionate oratory became the spear-carrier of the Dump Johnson effort—a movement with no staff and only a skeleton of antiwar mailing lists. Flying to a new town every day, he spoke to peace groups and students and "concerned Democrats" in Oregon and Wisconsin and wherever anyone could set up chairs. He was doggedly followed by Curtis Gans, who had left his staff job at ADA, and who now tried in each place to pull together some sort of functioning political structure in the wake of Lowenstein's inspiration. Back in New York, a law student named Harold Ickes spent his days and nights on the telephone, working with maniacal energy and humor to coordinate each little local and state committee into the semblance of a national organization.

This was the beginning of "the new politics" in 1968: a handful of young prophets-by-necessity in summer suits and clean-cut hair drumming up troops from the civil rights and peace movements and trying to connect them with the "doves" of the Democratic Party. They believed that the only way they could create an effective political effort against the war was to run a candidate for President on an antiwar platform. Ignoring the older liberals who wanted to concentrate on a "peace plank" at the 1968 Democratic Convention, they developed a grass-roots base for a Presidential candidacy, a network of people ready to open storefronts, answer phones, fill up rallies and generally take the place of a machine. It was possible for McCarthy to run for President only because the Dump Johnson nucleus had collected the power to issue an invitation.

3 THE DUMP JOHNSON ACTIVISTS DID NOT COME TO McCarthy first, nor did they come to him because he was their kind of politician. "He wasn't one of those liberals who believe in taking positions," I was told by a Washington lobbyist. "He never once alienated the establishment. He tried to work quietly behind the scenes."

McCarthy worked effectively, too, at first. As a Congressman he brought together a caucus of younger liberals who later became the Democratic Study Group, but who were known at first as "McCarthy's Marauders." McCarthy was respected for his intelligence and for his ability to unravel complicated economic bills. In the course of his ten years in the House, he was appointed to prestigious committee posts on the Banking and Currency and Ways and Means committees.

In the Senate, McCarthy was more retiring, partly because the senior Senator from Minnesota was Hubert Humphrey, a liberal who monopolized attention by both taking positions *and* working behind the scenes. McCarthy moved off-stage, and established good working relations with the southern powers in the Senate, especially Robert Kerr and Lyndon Johnson. Again he was placed on important committees, first Kerr's Finance Committee (chaired after Kerr's death by Russell Long), and later the Foreign Relations Committee.

In 1960 Senator McCarthy published *Frontiers in Ameri-*

can *Democracy*, his only book entirely written by himself. *Frontiers* is a philosophical essay on the structure of American democracy and the function of a liberal politician. Its theme is that the basic setup is a sound one, but requires constant adjustment if it is to serve the public good without unnecessarily restricting freedom. The perspective is that of an informed legislator who employs his "reasoned judgment" to work out balanced programs in accordance with the development of history. The process necessarily involves compromise, and McCarthy quotes Edmund Burke in appealing for public confidence in elected representatives, so that they may "act upon a varied and a large view of things." The job of a politician, as McCarthy quotes the Catholic philosopher Jacques Maritain, is "the mutable application of immutable moral principles even in the midst of the agonies of an unhappy world."

There is nothing in McCarthy's strictures about change coming through public movements or public pressure on government. He admires the New Deal because it was a "response to urgent practical demands," but he has nothing to say about the political form of those demands, and ends his chapter with a lecture that "the liberal is in danger of forgetting the obligations and restraints that are the price of freedom and of discounting the importance of institutions and their function in the perfecting of individual persons."

Nor is there any discussion of when and how a politician takes his case to the public. "The ideal politician is a good man, an informed man, and a man skilled in the art of politics"—but not, apparently, a leader of public activity. Since politics, in McCarthy's scheme of things, is the process of enlightened adjustment, there is no such a thing as a "cause." The belief in absolutes is properly confined to religion, and a politician who goes about "presenting himself like Carlyle's crusader as 'the minister of God's justice, doing God's judgment on the enemies of God'" has clearly fallen into "the devices of the demagogue."

Perhaps the greatest irony of 1968 is that a man whose political outlook was so rooted in the legislative process, in the accommodation of interests through restraint and compromise, in the preservation of the republic through balanced, gradual change, could have found himself at the head of a great popular movement. There are those in Washington who think that it might not have happened if McCarthy had not suffered a humiliation in the service of the institutions he respected and the leader who was a model of effectiveness.

4 IN 1964 SENATOR MCCARTHY WAS COMPETING WITH Hubert Humphrey to become Lyndon Johnson's Vice Presidential nominee. McCarthy wanted the job, and he allowed a campaign to be formed for him by Democrats who were unsympathetic to Humphrey and to Humphrey's backing, which came largely from organized labor. Even then, however, those who worked for McCarthy were frustrated by his inability to ask directly for support, or to make "a positive move" in his own behalf.

Although we didn't know it in 1968, McCarthy in 1964 was supported by the right wing of the Democratic Party: Richard Daley of Chicago, John Connally of Texas, Russell Long and other southern Senators, John McKeithen and other southern Governors. They stressed that McCarthy was the kind of person they could work with,* someone who was not identified in the South with civil rights, not indebted to the labor movement, and—for ticket-balancing purposes—a Catholic.

The campaign of course was directed at one voter: Lyndon Johnson, who kept McCarthy and Humphrey, as well as Thomas Dodd, dangling right up to convention time in Atlantic City. McCarthy resented being toyed with, and the Humphrey people in Minnesota had threatened opposition in McCarthy's upcoming senatorial primary if he didn't withdraw as a Vice Presidential candidate. From Atlantic City, McCarthy sent a telegram to the White House "commending" Humphrey for Vice President. Johnson still could have chosen McCarthy—if he were not Johnson, and if McCarthy had not released the telegram to the press.

The next day Johnson telephoned with the bad news. By coincidence, Arthur Goldberg was in the President's office, and after a few words with McCarthy, Johnson quickly handed Goldberg the phone. Years later, McCarthy was heard to say that "Goldberg and the liberal establishment" prevented his nomination as Vice President.

Walter Jenkins later called three times to ask McCarthy to nominate Humphrey. "Johnson didn't have the guts to ask me himself," said McCarthy. To Jenkins he said, "Tell Walter Reuther to nominate him!" But finally he agreed.

A White House aide later said that Johnson had wanted McCarthy and Humphrey to walk straight up to the platform

*Perhaps coincidentally, McCarthy during 1964 voted both in the Finance Committee and on the Senate floor against reducing the oil depletion allowance.

on either side of him, without either knowing who had been chosen. Then as the party and the country watched, Johnson would have turned to McCarthy and asked him to nominate Humphrey.

In 1960 McCarthy had made that dramatic speech nominating Stevenson for President—for reasons which may have had something to do with his regard for Lyndon Johnson. You would think that the Democratic Convention of 1964 would have wanted to listen to Gene McCarthy, but as he nominated Humphrey the delegates just went on talking; in fact, they started to leave while he was still speaking. "He stood up there," said a campaign assistant, "and you could see he was seething with anger and hurt."

5 THE CONSERVATIVE STYLE OF EUGENE MCCARTHY'S liberalism can be traced in part to his background and his education. German on his mother's side, McCarthy was raised and educated in the practically all-German area of Stearns and Meeker counties in rural Minnesota. Although McCarthy's forebears were there earlier, this area was settled mainly by Catholic immigrants who came in the last third of the nineteenth century—fugitives from Prussian conscription, from farm-blighting industrialism, and from the anti-Church purges of the *Kulturkampf*. The German Catholics were politically progressive, by and large, and gave strong support to Minnesota's farmer-labor movement.

They were also serious readers who quickly founded schools

and kept them up. Except for public high school and graduate study at the University of Minnesota, McCarthy's education was parochial and his later college teaching was confined to parochial Minnesota colleges. In McCarthy's area the schools were supervised by the Benedictines, one of the oldest and most tranquil of orders, who had avoided the "zeal" of scholasticism, the Counter Reformation, and the Catholic revival of the nineteenth century. In 1945, shortly before his marriage, McCarthy undertook an "eight or ten month" novitiate in a Benedictine monastery.

The German immigrants in the Midwest came quickly into conflict with the Irish-American hierarchy. The Germans looked down upon the Irish push toward "Americanism," as it was called in those days. Feeling that their religious community depended on the preservation of the German language and German customs, they stubbornly resisted the assignment of Irish priests and the teaching of English. As Peter M. Abbelen, a priest of the Archdiocese of Milwaukee, wrote in 1886: "The German Catholic—unlike the Irish—is surrounded by countrymen, who, as Protestants, Infidels, Secret-Society, may do everything in their power to allure him away from his Church." And at a convention of German Catholics in Chicago on September 7, 1887, a delegate from St. Paul rose to condemn the Knights of Labor by stating that "the Germans ought to consider it a disgrace to be ruled by Irish ignoramuses."

The pride in regulation and reserve, the scholastic superiority, the security in judging others who succumb to worldly experience, and, above all, the suspicion of things modern, industrial, and American: these left their mark on Gene

McCarthy, and on the temper he brought to the decisions of his campaign.

6 IF ONE HEARD McCARTHY'S STUMP TALKS DAY AFTER day, it was evident that his political vocabulary came directly from the tradition of Catholic social thought, which in the early Sixties had found its most progressive expression in the encyclicals of Pope John XXIII. This view of social action begins with the traditional notion that mortals will always be oppressed by their own evil, because their bodies are evil. "Consisting, as he does, of body and immortal soul," writes Pope John, "man cannot in this mortal life satisfy his needs or attain perfect happiness. Thus, the measures that are taken to implement the common good must not jeopardize his eternal salvation. Indeed, they must even help him to obtain it."

Despite the persistence of mortal imperfection, Catholic tradition teaches that there is an "order" in the universe which proclaims the glory of God, there are "laws" inscribed in man's nature, and there are "rights" which belong to every member of society. "Authority," too, "has its source in nature, and consequently has God for its author."

Senator McCarthy, as a religious person committed to this tradition, accepted what John called the "obligation" to act in behalf of social progress, so that man may achieve the greatest permissible degree of God's order. The principles of order are discovered by the exercise of "right reason," which

Senator McCarthy converted every day into "a politics of reason," using the word "reason" in exactly the way that Thomas Aquinas and Pope John used it—as that natural faculty which puts God in touch with man, which sets limits to authority and legitimizes action. As far back as the Humphrey nominating speech, he spoke of "our belief that the power of reason can give some direction to human life and some direction to the movement of history itself." "Reason" used in this sense is just about synonymous with "revelation."

When, in the Catholic tradition, a fallible human being would challenge authority, he may do so only after he has restrained his will and arrived at what McCarthy always called "a reasoned judgment." To act precipitously is to arouse violence and passion, and to destroy the good along with the bad. The proper pace for progress, in the words of Pope John, is "little by little."

To those who fail to perceive the divine guarantee of a higher order, the Church's call may seem lacking in a sense of immediacy. How does moving little by little toward a fuller degree of justice apply to those who are oppressed and dying *right now?* What does the acceptance of human imperfection prepare us to do about atrocities occurring right before our eyes? Can one act "little by little" to meet an emergency? And how does such a system deal with conflict? What if temporal authority finds it in its interests to put up a brick wall in the path of social justice?

Here was a basic difference between McCarthy and the volunteers who comprised "the McCarthy movement," which was in the main passionately secular. For McCarthy, all temporal conditions were relative. For the people who worked for him, their ends here on earth—peace in Vietnam, racial justice in America—were absolute.

Pope John tells us that "there are indeed some people who, in their generosity of spirit, burn with a desire to institute wholesale reforms. . . . They tackle the problem with such impetuosity that one would think they were embarking on some political revolution."

This is a perfect description of the McCarthy movement, whose workers really did desire a nonviolent revolution in America. Pope John, I think, would not have shown contempt for that burning desire, but Senator McCarthy often did. From the viewpoint of an obligation beyond space and time and flesh, there can be no such thing as an emergency. Therefore McCarthy despised the alarmists on his side as he despised the secularism of Robert Kennedy. "Our problem was too much help," he later told the *Boston Globe*. The most perfect way to raise a moral issue is to raise it all alone.

7 PERHAPS MCCARTHY REALLY WOULD HAVE LIKED TO carry out his campaign all by himself, if only the delegates stayed in the hall and did not ignore him. He would have liked it to be the example of his judgment and his reason that gave direction to America and changed the movement of history.

McCarthy's backers, as a rule, labored under a different conception of his candidacy. They wanted him to stand for critical changes in domestic and foreign policy, to lead their movement to a broader base, and at the proper moment to convert his popular strength into political power. Once they realized it was possible, all of these aims centered on the effort to make their candidate President. But for McCarthy, the race was over in a moral sense the day he agreed to run. With that act, he accepted his obligation and carried out his reasoned judgment. From then on, he tended to bury any criticism of himself beneath "the snows of New Hampshire."

For McCarthy, entering the primaries entailed no great obligation to the people trying to get him elected. His obligation was to raise certain issues, so that balance could be restored to the system. His notion had little to do with the collection and exercise of political power—but much to do with how one displayed one's personality. A candidate, to him, was he who shows in speech and action a proper expression of balanced judgment. Such an expression—for those who could understand it—would properly expose the hypocrisy and self-seeking of other candidates.

Such a candidate might bring the Democratic Party—which had gone askew under distorted leadership—to reflect the rightness and balance of his own personality. If he were truly deserving, and history were ripe, he might even be elected. In which case he would make an "adequate" President—which is all anyone can be and well beyond the reach of those who blow themselves to "greatness." History shows that power, said McCarthy again and again, is best exercised by those who do not seek it (which was pretty good politics, too, as long as he was running against Lyndon Johnson and Robert Kennedy). To seek power, he implied, would be to deform the character that made one worthy of power.

Thus McCarthy was reluctant to say he was running for President. He was "willing" to be President: he recognized that when one challenged the king, one should be prepared to take his place. This was modesty, we thought; of course, it was explained, he didn't really mean it.

But he did mean it, he was only "willing," and when the chips were down he made that all too clear. What reporters and others took as modesty or mystery or some form of concealment, of retreat from personality, was really personality itself, in such unfamiliar terms that most people just couldn't believe it. It took a while to sink in—and in the meantime, McCarthy made tough jokes about the various "interpretations" of himself in terms of political, temporal, selfish motives—like the motives of other candidates. To him these misunderstandings obscured the fundamental nature of his candidacy.

His original style was more than "form" to him, it was "substance"—to use two of his favorite scholastic words. It was a style that proved attractive to many and incomprehensible to many others. But that style was what McCarthy stood for, and it was the essence of everything he would not compromise.

So much depended, in the end, on McCarthy's personality. Movement or no, the qualities that made him what he was had a lot to do with bringing him so close to the White House. But in the end, these same qualities prevented him from leading the movement that bore his name, prevented that movement from having its fullest impact on American society.

For I believe, based on what I saw as one of his speechwriters from March to September, Wisconsin to Chicago, that McCarthy might have been President. Failing that, he might have given unity and direction to the major forces for progressive change in American life and government. He might have reached out to persuade millions of Americans who remained untouched by the issues which gave rise to his campaign. If I am right in this, his supporters need not talk about America failing them. There is a sense in which the McCarthy campaign failed America, and all who were part of it deserve a chance to think why.

8 PERSONALITY, TO BE SURE, IS MORE THAN PRINCIPLES and intentions; nor are principles and intentions all I mean when I speak of the McCarthy personality that so much depended on. Certainly Catholic idealism was not, in the final analysis, responsible for McCarthy. He was a man of mood who indulged his moods and expected others to indulge them. The patterns of his behavior were idiosyncratic in ways that no set of beliefs could fully account for. Perhaps it is well to set out in advance the qualities his campaign staff discovered as we went along.

Sometimes McCarthy's "restraint," his reluctance to act, was hard to distinguish from a fear of looking bad. In this he was not unlike certain athletes who would rather lose than go all-out to win. If one goes all-out and loses, then one is without excuse; everyone has clearly seen that the other man is better. But athletes who do not go all-out end up losing to anyone who is as good as they are and to some who are worse.

Likewise McCarthy seemed always to imagine the worst possible spectator's view of his motives. He had trouble, for example, approaching the leaders of ethnic groups and unions. It was as if their cause were not as important to him as the knowledge that, had he sought them out, it would have been matter-of-factly assumed he was advancing his own cause. The official explanation was that McCarthy was appealing to Americans as individuals, and not as groups. Still, he could have appealed to Americans as individuals to get behind, say, Cesar Chavez and the striking Mexican-American grape-pickers. When leaders *came to him,* McCarthy would pose with them and endorse their groups. But it was not in the man to approach others and open himself to criticism or rejection.

His instinct was to avoid confrontations, both personal and political. It was always explained by McCarthy's true believers that a given confrontation was avoided because it would only exacerbate tensions—but there were times when confrontations were clearly called for. It was an incongruous trait in a man celebrated for his courage, a trait that tested the believers ever more severely as the campaign wore on—and continually shifted discussion from McCarthy's ideas to his personality.

The voters and delegates could accept that personality or reject it—for, once having presented it, the candidate would remain passive. He would not put himself forward or strain at communication or ask directly for support. McCarthy's portrait of himself as a potential leader again was passive, stressing the propriety of his reactions rather than his capacity to initiate.

Again and again, he insisted on his personality, which

one had to swallow whole, on faith, not just in its principles but in its whims and moods. Criticism was impermissible, no matter its source or its quality. Though he laid great stress on constituencies and the obligation for elected leaders to respond to them, McCarthy seemed to feel that no one had a right to ask him to explain himself. Thus the man who was running on the issues demanded acceptance on total faith—which was one of the qualities for which we bitterly castigated LBJ.

Hardest to accept was a deep-seated bitterness, never quite accounted for by immediate circumstance, a bitterness which made him down-rate individuals, even as he was calling for a national policy of generosity.

McCarthy's contempt for excitement, his pessimism about the affairs of this earth, was expressed by a compulsive withdrawal that exceeded the limits of mere principle. Often when his supporters most strongly urged him to do something, he would either do it badly—and blame his advisers—or do the opposite, without explanation. If he were then criticized, if it was clear he had looked bad, he would withdraw further—do something against his immediate interests or those of his cause—as if to underscore that his inner values were not what his critics presumed and were not to be questioned.*

All of this added up at last to a man whose concept of his own identity was so precious to himself, and so fragile, that he could not tolerate disagreement or equality, could not, in fact, work directly and openly with others. It took a long

* When the Senate returned in 1968, McCarthy voted against Ted Kennedy in his successful effort to replace McCarthy's old comrade Russell Long as Democratic Whip. When McCarthy was criticized for the anti-Kennedy vote, he resigned his seat on the Foreign Relations Committee.

time to say it to ourselves. We would say it and take it back again. Certainly it was not the whole story. But toward the end one couldn't help wondering if there were not within McCarthy a reflex of guilt and fear so relentless that it demanded the destruction of every possibility of power or success.

9 IN NEW HAMPSHIRE, EVERYONE WAS ABJECTLY GRATEFUL to McCarthy just for entering. At last Johnson and Johnson's war were going to be challenged. It was forgivable, then, that the candidate was not going full throttle. It was laid to shyness, modesty, stiffness—all understandable in a man of such bearing and intelligence. Who could have explained at that point that worldly effort might lead to corruption, to the pressures of other people's expectations, perhaps to a showdown where one would be exposed and unbearably judged by common enthusiasts who had no right of judgment?

Yet it was frustrating, for those who cared, that much of the early campaign, before the final moments of New Hampshire, was vitiated by the candidate's reluctance to take practical responsibility for his spiritual decision. First of all, there was little interest in engaging a campaign staff. Curtis Gans and a few others who coordinated the New Hampshire campaign and brought in student canvassers were put on the payroll only at the last moment. McCarthy refused to phone more experienced people who were suggested for staff positions, and Blair Clark—a former newspaperman and CBS executive—was made campaign manager despite his own insistence that he was not a professional and must soon be replaced. McCarthy seemed to prefer nonprofessionals, who were shyer about bothering him. Blair Clark, for instance, stayed on as campaign manager till the end, and was instrumental, in fact, in McCarthy's decision to enter New Hampshire; while professionals who had worked for other candidates in the past were usually undermined and forced to quit the McCarthy effort. Three weeks before the New Hampshire primary, there was no campaign organization whatever. Thirteen offices had been opened in the state, but only three of them were staffed full-time. Back in Washington the mail piled up, the country was responding and for a long time there was no one even to open the envelopes.

The Dump Johnson managers were hoping the campaign would get off to a strong start on December 2, 1967, at the Conference for Concerned Democrats, where they had brought together Democratic politicians and officeholders from all over the country who were against the war. They were hoping McCarthy would announce his candidacy on that occasion, but he announced two days earlier in Washington. At the conference in Chicago, he insisted on sharing the platform with no one, though the organizers had hopes to make a show of support and strength. When McCarthy was late, Al Lowenstein spoke to hold the audience, and McCarthy was angry at him for speaking strongly. He shrank from Lowenstein's personal attack on Johnson—he had deep misgivings about a group of young rebels using him as a battering-ram against his party. McCarthy himself spoke with no particular substance or feeling, and afterwards refused to visit the overflow crowd of four thousand who had waited downstairs for three hours. He said he thought he had done enough; the organizers had to say he didn't know the people were down there.

McCarthy's attitude then and later was that he was doing his supporters a favor by "letting them use my name." Understandably, he had reservations about their inexperience and optimism. He knew as well as anyone that their purposes and values were not necessarily his. But it was all the more incongruous that he left it up to them to propose a campaign, and took the attitude that he for his part would accept whatever of it he could bear. At one point he agreed to a TV interview on *Face the Nation* only if his schedulers would cancel two days of New Hampshire.

Though it frustrated his campaign staff, McCarthy's demeanor was a great advantage with the young people who began to come to him in New Hampshire, mainly from the elite colleges of the East Coast and the upper West Side of New York City. The students enjoyed McCarthy's respectability and wit as the outer signs of solidity, courage and wisdom. They didn't miss his not directing them: he was the permissive father who is really wonderful but who has to be explained to outsiders. And it seemed *he trusted them* to do the explaining. Unlike their real parents, he saw (they thought) that action belongs to youth, that "the new generation" is really going to save the world.

The dedication and seriousness of the students who canvassed for McCarthy was not only legendary but real. They truly were, as Robert Kennedy was later to point out, the "A" students in their high schools and colleges. Politically they were inclined to some romanticization of the NLF, Chè Guevara, and Malcolm X. But whether they came with beards to shave or not, these were kids who reacted against the violent anti-Americanism of the New Left, whom they far outnumbered. Though they hated the war and the draft, they still believed that America could be beautiful—if it would live up to its own principles. American optimists at heart, immune in the long run to ideology, they were terribly grateful to have a chance to do something real. Most of them had thought that chance would never come.

The campaign headquarters set up in Concord, a good safe 20 miles from the more indolent atmosphere of the candidate's entourage at the Wayfarer ski lodge in Manchester. Joel Feigenbaum and Matty Bornstein, a couple of graduate physics students from Cornell, set the canvassing process into motion with a statistical analysis of New Hampshire's population and political distribution—a technique they employed later on in Portland, Oregon. Another young academic named Ben Stavis divided New Hampshire into maps and charts by which he could keep precise accounts of the canvassing. A telephone system tracked ward-by-ward progress and routed incoming volunteers. By the last week, the young managers were turning volunteers away. They rang the doorbell of every Democrat and independent in the state—some two or three times. On the day before the election they delivered to every house a sample ballot marked with McCarthy's 24 electors.

I have heard tapes of some of the door-to-door conversations in New Hampshire and Wisconsin: the best of them were conducted in a tone of respect which must have surprised both parties. The canvassers were learning more than they were teaching—learning that whether or not people understood Vietnam, they knew that something had gone very wrong with this country. The canvassers had been instructed not to argue but to ask questions and let people talk. Often the voters fumbled with personal discontents, burst out with hatred that transcended its immediate objects—but many, many connected their troubles with Lyndon Johnson, and some, amazingly, said just about what the kids were saying. The canvassers could then suggest to them a look at Gene McCarthy. A look would convince you he was a serious, honest, careful person—if he were President, people would come back to America again, just as we have. People could talk again, just as we're talking now.

That was the mood, at least. The McCarthy kids loved McCarthy, they loved each other, they loved New Hampshire and Wisconsin. No wonder Bobby Kennedy admired them: it takes a hard case to turn away from love. Especially when the lovers are smart and young and healthy.

Yet we will never know if the canvassing won a significant number of votes directly. Perhaps its chief value was the kind of publicity it gave McCarthy as the man who had brought our young people "back into the system." This probably wouldn't have worked as well for Robert Kennedy, whose youthful demeanor created too close an identification with enthusiasm and irresponsibility. But McCarthy's gravity safely set him apart from the students, even as their decency and commitment were credited to his influence.

Granting the students' effectiveness one way or another, it can hardly be said that McCarthy's success in New Hampshire was due to a spontaneous popular uprising. From the beginning he had the help of a group of New Hampshire Democrats who were shrewd in directing ads and publicity to the local taste. McCarthy himself was made visible by a good amount of money put into simple, straightforward TV spots. And on February 23, Richard Goodwin drove into the lodge, having stopped en route for dinner with Bobby Kennedy, and added his energy and experience to the handful of intimidated novices who composed McCarthy's campaign staff. Goodwin brought a certain amount of prestige and publicity simply by being there. He was always doing things, and was better than anyone else at getting the candidate to do things, too. He even got McCarthy to say he was running for President when he taped his TV ads.

Goodwin was not Kennedy's agent; Kennedy, in fact, did not approve of his coming. Goodwin came because he was against the war, because he knew Johnson could be beat, and because he wanted to be in on the action. He had written in *The New Yorker* in the fall of 1967 (under the pseudonym "Bailey Laird") a political fantasy in which he predicted that Lyndon Johnson could easily be beaten. He had argued consistently for Robert Kennedy to make the race, only to find himself opposed by nearly all the other old Kennedy pros, especially by his longtime rival, Ted Sorensen. When Bobby refused, Goodwin set out to do his best for McCarthy.

From the day he came, Goodwin proclaimed to anyone who would listen that Johnson was beaten—and that McCarthy was a better candidate than anyone thought.

Johnson had lost America. The question that brought the gleam to Goodwin's deep, cobwebbed eyes was, who would win it?

10 I GOT MY FIRST GLIMPSE OF McCARTHY FIFTEEN DAYS before New Hampshire, when some wealthy backers arranged a cocktail party at a posh town house in Manhattan. There were carefully collected show-business people, arts and writing people, rich people: come with curiosity and a bit of trepidation. Most were in despair at the reluctance of Kennedy. Because for all their foppery and fashionability, they were genteel people deeply disturbed about the war and the cities, yearning for someone who might tell them what to do, who might take their talent and influence and money and put it to use to save their country.

McCarthy looked grave and weary. Eventually he made a little talk with allusions to poets, expressing his sense of the country's divisions. The President could not travel openly, he commented. But one's mind wandered. The living room was pop art, like a child's bedroom, full of costumed jugglers, skinny, pretty, sitting on the rug. McCarthy had got there by mistake. He looked over our heads as he spoke, an old teacher reading an old lecture from the roof of his mind. When he finished, they took him off right away. No one asked for names or time or money. The celebrities shrugged, and gossiped of Kennedy.

Before that, Robert Lowell had supplied a rambling introduction. "You're supposed to be artists," he said to the beautiful people. "I don't see many artists here." But his audience knew better—they had signed the artists' and writers' petition against the war. Finally Lowell turned to the candidate, who sat behind him in an antique chair. "You haven't got a chance, you know that, don't you?"

McCarthy sat motionless, his face set, his eyes to Lowell with no expression, no acknowledgment. The room was silent. No one spoke, not even the official backers. Lowell resumed his introduction with grim satisfaction. What on earth were we doing there?

There were always writers and columnists who cherished McCarthy as a loser. He verified their literary conception of America, reinforced their burden of irony. They were pleased when he nearly won New Hampshire, elated when Lyndon fell, but Chicago was best of all for them. If McCarthy had really won in the end, they would never have forgiven him.

11

POLLSTERS AND POLITICIANS HAD SAID AT FIRST THAT McCarthy would do well to win 10 percent. When all the votes were counted—including Republican write-ins—McCarthy came within several hundred votes of defeating the President in hawkish New Hampshire. Richard Goodwin saw McCarthy "go through an almost physical change, you could see the color come into his face," as he stood and took the cheers of his supporters on election night. He must have known then that he was not going to embarrass himself—he was going to be a genuine candidate for the Presidency.

Yet the moral victory in New Hampshire intensified McCarthy's problem with his campaign. All around him—at every rally, on every campus, in every campaign storefront—he could see the faces of men and women who wanted a rapid and thorough change in American government—people who had little respect for "obligations and restraints" or "the importance of institutions" such as the U.S. Senate. They now celebrated Eugene McCarthy as "a breath of fresh air"—a personal symbol for a national transformation to come as easily and as happily as success in New Hampshire. Making oneself a symbol had been the essence of demagoguery to McCarthy—that was why he had tried to work "effectively" in Congress—that was one of the qualities that set him apart, in his own mind, from, say, Robert Kennedy.

Soon that very Robert Kennedy would be entering the race, and McCarthy knew that Robert Kennedy would not hesitate to make himself a symbol—to act as if he came riding on a white horse, personally to solve the country's problems one by one. The entry of Kennedy was sure to increase the tension in the political atmosphere, which was already severe. As McCarthy had written in *Frontiers of Democracy*, "The Christian in politics should shun the devices of the demagogue at all times, but especially in a time when anxiety is great, when tension is high, when uncertainty prevails, and emotion tends to be in the ascendancy."

The kids and the liberals were idolizing him, and McCarthy knew he was not exactly what they believed he was. Yet he must have thought, too, that the applause was not undeserved—he had had little enough of it in his career. He would continue, with restraint; he rejected an overture from the Kennedys. He would have to go ahead in his own way, saying what he thought was right, in the belief that those who could see, would see. They would see an example of how a President should conduct himself. Regardless of what anyone thought or anyone said, an example was not the same as a symbol.

12

AMERICAN POLITICS WOULD NEVER BE QUITE THE SAME after New Hampshire. First of all, there was the fact that a candidate of no prior national fame had shaken an incumbent President without established backing and without a political machine. If McCarthy had done only that, *dienu!* We would be forever grateful. There could be such a thing as issue politics on the Presidential level, the war in Vietnam was such an issue, and when amateurs got together in a certain spirit, even the President had better look out! Regardless of what happened thereafter, we had the suspicion that democracy could be made to work. No matter who was President, we would know that government could never be quite the closed room we had feared it was. There was a point where history simply was not going to absolve a President. There was a point where ordinary people could make a little history of their own.

And the Johnson people had made it even sweeter for us by raising the issue of patriotism. A McCarthy victory would bring joy in Hanoi, they informed the public. Governor King said that McCarthy was "a champion of appeasement and surrender." Senator McIntyre said that McCarthy was good news for "draft-dodgers and deserters." They ran newspapers ads telling how Ho Chi Minh was counting on McCarthy in New Hampshire.

All of this only underscored the unprecedented nature of McCarthy's challenge. He had run against an American war while that war was going on. He was more than a General Eisenhower who promised peace with military prestige. He was a dove who asked whether the price of victory was worth it.

If you did it right, if you did it with McCarthy's kind of dignity, you could emerge with your reputation untarnished. And there was much to be said here for the self-imposed discipline of the youth corps. "Clean for Gene" was a policy of practical political sophistication. For several years the peace movement had been having a mixed effect on America. In New Hampshire it was possible for students to work effectively against the war and the assumptions behind the war without an exchange of hostility.

For McCarthy had begun to do much more than simply advocate peace. He was, to his lasting credit, the first Presidental candidate directly to challenge the American military and its role in the decision-making process. McCarthy did not invent this challenge from scratch: his comments fit into an increasing trend of criticism which he himself had been part of with his attacks from the Senate floor on foreign arms sales and the unchecked activities of the CIA. Other Senators, such as William Fulbright and George McGovern, had played more prominent roles in the burgeoning assault on the Pentagon; there were figures in national life, though not in Congress, who had made telling connections between the military and the American corporate economy. But it was McCarthy's singular achievement to develop an acceptable public diction for a criticism of American policy which up till then had been expressed only in a limited, academic context or in terms which the public rejected as eccentrically radical.

I shall spell out this diction in Section 15. The point here is that the McCarthy campaign legitimized open and extensive attack on the military by respectable politicians, who learned in 1968 that it would not necessarily kill their public careers. In the Congress of 1968–69, for instance, there has been full-scale opposition to the Nixon-backed anti-ballistic missile proposal, including an open challenge to the Pentagon's reliability and honesty. Senator Edward Kennedy, among others, has gone further on this issue than either he or his brother were willing to venture before 1968. Clearly we have come some distance from the days when Congress merely rubber-stamped the Pentagon. McCarthy was not the only leader in this process. But he was the first to judge that the issue could be presented in a national campaign, and the first to find a way to do it.

For all of these achievements, McCarthy's conservative manner and lack of zeal were a political asset. He put his criticisms into a context of restoring institutions rather than transforming them. Thus he was able to criticize the government without scaring people with plans for structural change. On this score, his analysis and his vocabulary did not go to the roots of America's social and political crisis. McCarthy spoke always of restoring balance rather than creating a new sort of society in America. The great paradox of his candidacy is that this approach had the political impact to give hope once more to those who believed that only deep changes could save their country.

Since McCarthy himself didn't see it that way, it was inevitable that there would come a time when his actions as a candidate would not match the expectations of his most active supporters. In the final analysis, their picture of the world was not his, and his purposes could not be harnessed with their potential. In the meantime, McCarthy and his troops had given each other much to rejoice about, and much to do.

13 I JOINED THE CAMPAIGN IN WISCONSIN. BEFORE I ARrived Goodwin complained I was "too radical," but changed his mind when he saw how quickly he could teach me to write what I later identified as a Kennedy-style speech. A Kennedy speech begins with a terrible problem: sluggish economy, shortage of medical care, water pollution, old people, federal neglect of Wisconsin. We got pages of statistics from our Harvard-MIT student-researchers, condensed them to a couple of paragraphs of well-bred outrage. Look at this, look at that. A country like the United States, we can do better. We've got to stop this war and get ourselves moving again. We conclude with some snappy Kennedy-style programs, one-two-three. More hospitals, more day-care centers, regional planning, foster grandparents. Then rush the speech down to McCarthy, who cut it to its bones. Next day he might get one or two sentences into his usual stump talk. It would be mimeographed as a statement and appear in the Wisconsin newspapers.

It was enough to be part of something, though personally I was more impressed by what I saw at the canvassing headquarters in the basement of the dumpy Wisconsin Hotel, four blocks downhill from Milwaukee's ornate Sheraton-Schroeder where McCarthy stayed with his immediate staff. Most of the 13,000 canvassers were students, with a sprinkling of housewives and people in their late twenties. But the captains and lieutenants were young groomed professional people in vests and loosened ties, who had the state of Wisconsin divided into detailed battle maps. Around the clock they greeted the waves of canvassers, briefed them concisely, and directed them to new target areas. Since Republicans could cross over in Wisconsin, their objective was to ring every doorbell in the state. They had sixteen days, and they made it with days to spare. The officers here were from the "silent generation" which slipped through college in the fifties. (I myself hit the tail end of it with the class of '58.) Most of them had become teachers or technicians of one sort or another. Now they were brought out from isolated expertise into the kind of political activity which had never before seemed meaningful or even possible to them. Perhaps they were beginning to claim their fair share of the power. If people of their class and education felt strongly about ending the war and establishing certain social priorities, they would hardly be denied their voice in government.

At the Sheraton-Schroeder, a mad joy prevailed. Kids on the McCarthy press corps worked all night on peanut butter, getting out transcripts and information. Managers held meetings all day long, researchers rushed up corridors in their underwear, everyone stayed up drinking and talking and fooling around. We were heady with history, which we knew was driving us on to win in Wisconsin.

But one day I was surprised to find a knot of young

campaign workers assaulting Campaign Coordinator Curt Gans and some local Democratic managers because McCarthy had not gone to the Milwaukee ghetto. Going to the ghetto seemed largely symbolic to me at the time. McCarthy was on the right side of the issue; in 1959–60 he had chaired the Senate Special Committee on Unemployment, which issued a 4,000-page report citing the same facts as the Kerner Commission did in 1968 and making many of the same recommendations. Now McCarthy was calling the Kerner Report the most important public document of the century; he was the only candidate to call for its full implementation. I thought the main job was to beat Johnson in Wisconsin; and it was not surprising that McCarthy would be wary of high-powered ghetto tours which meant little in substance and which could not help him in the numerous wards of white workers.

In the middle of Wisconsin, however, McCarthy's press secretary, Sy Hersch, who had been with McCarthy every day since before New Hampshire, and Hersch's top assistant, Mary Lou Oates, resigned, largely because of the way they were personally undermined, but also because of the ghettos, a fact which was played up in *The New York Times*. After that McCarthy did stride through the ghetto, on a cold day when not many people were in the streets, moving at a fast lope which gave him the pleasure of winding the press and TV people. Three black boys playing basketball in a schoolyard looked up and saw a mob of shouting white people bearing down on them. They ran.

McCarthy then gave a speech on the race problem—in the Sheraton-Schroeder ballroom, to an audience of his young white followers brought up specially from the Wisconsin

Hotel and looking scruffy but honored among the rows of neat dull reporters restless for lack of "news." The speech was good, though too general to make anybody's front pages. The kids applauded, and McCarthy, for the moment, was in the clear. Wisconsin was good to him, and in every college town his people turned out to meet him, chanting "Peace! Peace! Peace!"

14 McCARTHY'S SPEECHES ARE WORTH SOME PARTICULAR attention here. To understand them properly one must know the basic facts of campaign oratory. As a rule, speechwriters do not write much of what a candidate says. They write only the "text" portion which is designed to make news each day and which is released in advance to the press. No candidate has time to compose serious, documented statements in the middle of campaigning, but candidates usually confer with their writers and carefully edit what they are going to have to stand behind. National reporters then add an extra check by their reluctance to quote from advance texts unless the candidate actually speaks them.

Depending on the candidate and the occasion, texts can be important. What he stands and falls on every day, however, are the interchangeable parts of his stump speech, which he develops much as a stand-up comedian develops his "bits." Each "bit" is a piece of comment centered around fixed phrases suggested by an adviser or thought up by the candidate himself. The candidate tries out the "bit"; if it goes over, he expands it. He is constantly adding, dropping, and recombining "bits" to suit the changing circumstances of his campaign.

The bits composing McCarthy's stump speech are worth reconstruction here, partly because he did not consistently use texts until he got to Oregon, and even then he usually surrounded them with his own bits and often embellished the texts as he read them. (The average reporter, who has to be fed with a spoon, could not follow the embellishments and would quickly conclude that McCarthy had abandoned his text.) In McCarthy's case his stump speech was doubly significant because of his conception of campaigning. What he repeated each day was the expression of his personality and the essence of what he was offering the American people in 1968.

In Oregon and California every day and on through the summer several times a week, McCarthy read texts addressed to particular issues and to problems of specific groups. But he didn't like it. Particularly he didn't like to speak of "the details" of a problem, which he knew could be lined up however a politician wished. Nor was he happy proposing specific programs, because who can really know in advance what steps he will have to take if he finds himself in office? His main desire was to present his values, express his sense of obligation, and let the public vote confidence or not.

God knows, if one examines carefully the "programs" of the other candidates of 1968, one will find them in the main a hodgepodge collection of shallow, makeshift, contradictory stuff. Whatever his shortcomings in terms of specifics or in terms of leadership, McCarthy offered a consistent political analysis and emerged from the campaign as the only candidate who could not be quoted against himself.

When the mood was good and the audience adoring, McCarthy spoke with marvelous fluency, subtlety and wit. Even on routine occasions, he spoke spontaneously in near-perfect periods, but with an excess of qualification and a lack of emphasis that usually lost his audience. There was a fine line between solemn listening and dreaming at a McCarthy speech not unlike the line which exists in college lecture classes—but it was impressive all the same to see solemn listeners at political rallies. The nonenthusiast, half-hearing an average speech, would never believe McCarthy at his best. Those eerie, unpredictable moments—at the Pfister Hotel in Milwaukee in March, Oregon State University in May, outdoors in a dark meadow on a hot August night in Houston—would kindle and rekindle the hope that the man was saving it for the right moment, that when it really counted—and only he would know—he would step up and lay it on the line for America.

Until that happy day, here is a reconstruction of McCarthy's stump speech. I have tried to include all the important "bits"; naturally there are more of them in my reconstruction than there were on any actual occasion. But the substance, I believe, is pure McCarthy.

15 He had entered as a test of the democratic process, calling upon the people to pass judgment on the war, on our involvement in that war, on the question of priorities, and on the future role of America. The last Presidential election had not been a test; 1964 was a year of non-politics, Lyndon Johnson *vs.* a dream world where the clocks have no hands, the calendars no numbers, and "the pale horse of death and the white horse of victory are indistinguishable." In 1968, then, Johnson's policies and the assumptions behind them had to be "taken to the people."

McCarthy allowed he had taken chances—but he joked that most of his political future was behind him anyway. 1968 was a year which called for taking chances (an allusion to Robert Kennedy). His student followers had taken the risk of leaving their studies. They, too, were trying to make the process work (as they had not before McCarthy).

Always he would mention "the snows of New Hampshire." It was cold there in the valleys, and we were all alone. He saw others up on the mountaintops lighting bonfires, but they had not come down where the action was.

There were no leaders, really, in his campaign. It was a "Children's Crusade," and if the original had had the people he had, it would have gone "all the way to Jerusalem." After Wisconsin, when reporters began to use the Crusade image slightingly, McCarthy addressed his young followers as "the government in exile . . . ready to go back in power."

He said he had been patient about the war, he had "reserved judgment." He had tried, at first, to believe his government. But it had become clear that the war was no longer defensible—"militarily, diplomatically, economically—or morally." (Crescendo to a great cheer on that last word.) The war had not gained the support of "what is generally accepted as the decent opinion of mankind."

One of the reasons the war had escaped "public review," was that the power of the Pentagon and the CIA had grown beyond "civilian control"—such as he and his colleagues were trying to establish through the Senate Foreign Relations Committee. The Pentagon had interfered in foreign affairs through "military missions in half the countries of the globe" and through unchecked arms sales. The CIA had committed U.S. interests through their clandestine encouragement of "counter-insurgency" groups. He found the effects of a "militarized" foreign policy in the invasion of Cuba, the Dominican intervention, "the quick support which we give to most military takeovers in Latin America," and in "what prepared the way for the military junta in Greece."

"If elected," McCarthy said, "I would go to the Pentagon."

He then would do a routine on how whatever the Church was dropping, the Pentagon was picking up: ". . . the idea of Grace of Office, as if to say, 'The Secretary of State knows better.' The ideas of Infallibility, of a Holy War, of Heresy. And the beginnings of an Inquisition. Even a kind of index called 'sanitizing the records.' I said the real danger point would come when they began to speak Latin in the Pentagon. I saw some very distressing signs of it. More and more, the words they used had rather strong Latin roots . . . words like 'pacification,' 'escalation.' Then there was a report that the Army had signed a contract with Douglas Aircraft to do a study of something called 'Pax Americana.' That, I think was the last bit of evidence that they had gone too far."

McCarthy would offer a thumbnail history of how the U.S. had taken up a position against "the movement of history" in Vietnam: because we had honored "the dead hand of the past" in "some kind of vague commitment" signed by John Foster Dulles "fifteen or twenty years ago"; because Walt Rostow theorized that the country stood at the middle of a great East-West balance; because Dean Rusk had visions of one billion Chinese armed with nuclear weapons by the year 2000—which was his first acknowledgement that China existed. Larry O'Brien, as Postmaster under Johnson, had actually announced that if General Marshall were alive, he would be supporting the war in Vietnam. Now that O'Brien had quit the White House to campaign for Robert Kennedy, McCarthy wondered if he had "kept open his lines of communication." (He didn't comment when O'Brien later returned to Humphrey, presumably bringing the ghost of Marshall along with him.)

The trouble with these people was that they put the United States into a defensive posture—as indicated by the very name, Department of Defense. McCarthy thought that as the world's strongest country, we could afford to "make mistakes on the side of trust rather than mistrust, generosity rather than fear and suspicion toward our fellow citizens and toward the rest of the world." He quoted Roosevelt on "the fear of fear."

McCarthy pointed out that the war was also unsound fiscally. For the first time in history, rumors of peace would send the stock market up instead of down—which contradicted Marxist theories of the business cycle and was a tribute to the way we had learned to manage the economy. There were politicians and economists who hated to give up the business cycle—but nonetheless, war was no longer a boost to the economy.*

McCarthy would begin his discussion of racial problems by comparing Negroes in America to "a kind of colonial

*McCarthy never mentioned corporate involvement in defense policy, or how the banks and corporations lay the financial weight of the war on the back of the working man—but neither did other candidates.

nation living in our midst"—not very different from the former colonies of European nations. Rather than addressing the colonial nation, McCarthy spoke to America at large, in terms of what we must do to allow the people of the colony "full participation in the good life of America."

McCarthy had heard that Kennedy had set up "twenty-six separate committees to deal with twenty-six varieties of Americans—like twenty-six varieties of ice cream"—as if one could put groups together for political purposes "like a jigsaw puzzle." This was not, to McCarthy, "the real America"; it was "not organic, not vital, not alive." "Respecting each person," he would address himself to all Americans as individuals: "a constituency of conscience."

What conscience demanded for the Negroes was the "four new civil rights" McCarthy had adapted in 1959 from Franklin D. Roosevelt's State of the Union Address of 1944. He would preface them with an encyclical definition of civil rights as arising "not from documents and laws" but from "a kind of philosophical inquiry really as to what is the nature of man—and from a reading of history." Thus he talked about the "accepted" rights of voting, trial by jury, privacy, freedom of person, public education, etc., as conditions which were considered at a given time and place to be "vital and necessary to the full life of the person and having some bearing on the good society."

The four new rights for our time turned out to be (1) "the right to not just any kind of job, but a job which returns a decent living"; (2) "the right to an education related to one's potential to learn" ("Head Start, and late start, and even middle start" was as specific as McCarthy ever got on this subject); (3) "the right to adequate health, to some measure of physical security"; (4) "the right to a decent house, not a house in isolation, not a house in a ghetto, but a house in a neighborhood which is part of a community which must be a part of the United States of America."

It must be a matter of priority for this country to change the conditions which created riots—as outlined in the Kerner Report—so that citizens need not exercise superhuman virtue simply to be good citizens.

Later in the campaign, McCarthy took this one step further. "If you go around for two hundred years," he said, "talking about a land of opportunity, you can't be surprised when people begin to protest and demonstrate. If politicians go around talking about the productive capacities of this country, you should not be surprised if there's a march of poor people on Washington.

"And if you ask people to be responsible," he added, "you can't be surprised when people stand up in an election year and say, 'We have passed a moral judgment and we want to see that judgment reflected in action.' And if you deplore the young people leaving the system, you can't be surprised when they do come in and demand a voice."

Placing his own candidacy in the context of popular demands, McCarthy would insist that "in pursuing this office I am not fulfilling any boyhood dream of mine. You have some politicians who look at the White House and say, 'That's where I want to live.' I haven't said that. I never thought that. In fact, I think it should be made into a museum. Nor could I say that I have any claim on it by succession."

McCarthy would recall that in nominating Stevenson in 1960, he had said that "Power is best exercised by those who are sought out by the people, by those to whom power is given by a free people. . . . And the seeking of me as a candidate came like the dew in the night. It was rather gentle, I must say, soft, but there were signs in the morning that something had happened during the night, and so here we are."

Just as a President must not seek the Presidency, neither must he "personalize" the office. He must not speak, as Johnson spoke, of "my" country, "my" Cabinet, or "my" Vice President. The office properly belongs "not to the man who holds it but to the people of this nation," and it therefore must be exercised "by the will of the majority" and "for the good of the entire nation."

Yet we have "a government of men as well as laws," and therefore J. Edgar Hoover, General Hershey, and Dean Rusk would have to be fired, for each of them had abused the functions of his office.*

McCarthy wanted to replace the abuses of government with "a new kind of politics," but he was as lame as most other commentators in trying to describe it: "a politics which says that decisions will not be made in smoke-filled rooms . . . that decisions will not be accepted out of a false sense of loyalty to one's party, a politics that says we will not be frightened off because someone is likely to charge . . . that we are disloyal or living on the edge of treason." McCarthy offered no specifics on ways and means to increase popular participation in government. In conclusion he would be reduced to something like, "The new kind of politics says that

*McCarthy's conservative framework permitted him a kind of plain speaking here which no other candidate would have dared—and his targets were bulwarks of hawkery and super-patriotism. But the definitive concept again was personality: all whom McCarthy criticized were leaders who were in one way or another defective in relation to basically sound institutions.

we must use the power of reason to make some judgment upon both life and history."

He was the first candidate in 1968 to invoke the need for a murky "reconciliation": "a reconciliation of the young and the old, of labor and management, and farmers and businessmen, of the academic community with the society as a whole, a reconciliation of race with race, a reconciliation of the Congress with the Presidency, and even of the Secretary of State with the Foreign Relations Committee."

Toward the end McCarthy would refer to a new spirit abroad in the land, a revival of "the spirit described by John Adams [or sometimes John Quincy Adams] as one of 'public happiness' [and later appropriated by Humphrey as 'the politics of joy'], which, said Adams, possessed the American colonists and won the Revolution even before it was fought, a spirit which was reflected in a delight in participation, in public discussion and in public action, a joy in citizenship, in self-government, in self-control, in self-discipline and in dedication."

His favorite end-quote was from "I Hear America Singing" by Walt Whitman, a rhapsodic rendering of the carpenter, the mason, the boatman, the mother, the young wife, etc.—all singing as they go about their business, "Each singing what belongs to him or her, and to none else."

Whitman concluded by addressing the next generation:

> Poets to come! Orators, singers, musicians to come—
> Not to-day is to justify me, and answer what I am for;
> But you, a new brood, native, athletic, continental, greater
> than before known.

"He was speaking of us," McCarthy said. "And then he said —and this must be our theme: 'Arouse! Arouse—for you must justify me—you must answer.' "

16 ON MARCH 31, 1968, AS I LAY ON THE FLOOR NEARLY sleeping, Teddy White appeared, drifting across the room with his hand outstretched toward the TV screen. "Johnson snapped," he said. "His nerve snapped."

Goodwin was gurgling, "We've won, we've won! I thought he wouldn't fold for two months more!"

Our canvassers had had us up to 64 percent, but we didn't believe it, we were afraid to release that figure. If Johnson hadn't dropped, Wisconsin would have gone that way, and he would have lost forever his chance for newspaper statesmanship. The slop about Lady Bird and the ranch—forget it! Even with sympathy for Johnson, a last-minute radio and phone campaign, and an anticlimax at the polls, Wisconsin went 56 to 35 for McCarthy.

McCarthy was speaking in a small-town auditorium when suddenly the reporters rushed the stage. "I felt like Orestes pursued by the Furies," he said that night.

"It's a whole new ball game," Goodwin said. He was eager for McCarthy to call some politicians—beginning with Chicago's Richard Daley.

McCarthy was feeling good, he really did make a few calls. But he kept the press waiting for two hours in the ballroom while he gave an exclusive interview on local TV. Then he told them what he loves most to tell people: there was nothing to get excited about.

Next day he had a half-hour on national TV, with America tuned in to see the man who knocked out Johnson. Goodwin and others had hoped that a rally could be staged, with McCarthy speaking strongly on his conception of leadership for America. McCarthy, however, turned the show over to old friends from his Minnesota ad agency, who brought the camera in tight and let him ramble on without a text, just as he used to do back in Minnesota, giving the blandest parts of his stump speech. He couldn't sustain it, no one can, the gaze of the big eye is cruel. He stumbled, cracked a false laugh, and dragged in limping. But the farmers upstate loved it, and the rest of the country, well, they could see he was sincere and then snap off with no damage done. Except that he hadn't really addressed them.

Downstairs in the Sheraton-Schroeder there was dancing and singing the night Lyndon snapped. But in the bar I met some assistant professors from Madison hunched darkly over their drinks. They'd got a war referendum on the ballot there, but it called for unilateral withdrawal, and it was not going to win. In their anger and depression they could see at once I'd been taken in. Johnson could come back, don't you see, that was without a doubt his plan. Besides, it's not Johnson who makes the war; it is the institutions of this country. Right, but people matter, I say. It matters who is President. I think. Still they were inconsolable without Lyndon.

17 THAT AFTERNOON I HAD SEEN NIXON IN THE GRAND ballroom. Neat little sexless women in stewardess dresses were bustling about with hot liquids and airplane hors d'oeuvres. They had unfolded a series of portable wooden ramps, leading back and forth across the ballroom until they ascended in front to the stage, where Nixon stood with Pat and Tricia and Julie and David shaking hands all afternoon like a row of wind-up dolls, smiling and unsmiling so that each smile might be new. Mrs. Nixon tilted from side to side as she rocked two steps and back again with each warm shake 'n' smile.

The pale clean people stood quietly in the pens all afternoon, soothed by the slow movement of the line through its wooden channel.

Nixon was nearby in every state, discreetly milking scrubbed white hands of a Sunday while we fought our epic battles. One didn't read much about him. On the road to the airport we'd see the billboards where he looked studiously into his open briefcase. But we were fighting for the real and the true, and we ignored him.

18 THE NIGHT HE WON, MCCARTHY MADE A BRIEF TRIP to the Wisconsin Hotel to visit his troops. He told them about Jerusalem and they cheered him, cheering themselves;

then he moved through them with his valet walking behind him to ward off arms and hands. Listening and talking were out of the question. There was no contact from bottom to top in the campaign for a politics of participation; the candidate did pretty much what he pleased, listening as a rule only to those with money or persistence enough to impose on him.

We knew that night that Johnson was beaten in Wisconsin, we knew more or less who had beat him: McCarthy and his people, the shadow of Bobby, and the Tet offensive. What bothered those people who bothered to think of it was the problem of who had won.

Exactly who, after all, was represented by us? To whom was our candidate responsible? It was clear that despite his strong critique of the military, McCarthy's respect for the balance of existing institutions—and more than that, his conservation of feeling and energy—pleased businessmen and suburban Republicans. They were voting against this particular war, but were they voting to change America? The racial issue, for instance, had not been clearly put. McCarthy's Minnesota agency wanted him never to mention race. And the working-class wards of Milwaukee had gone for Johnson.

With what right, then, did our youth corps proclaim that Wisconsin had voted for a new kind of politics? In whose name did we say that the primaries proved America's desire for change?

Some left at this juncture, a few to Kennedy, most to stay neutral. But a majority of the younger people stayed on with McCarthy, and dissolved their doubts into a determination to trust the man and win for him. It was hard to step back when already you were part of history. We had done one good thing, one big thing—that nobody could deny. McCarthy had to be good, or how could we be so good? The important thing was to make him President. We would justify him—that would be our answer. Or else the beauty of our love and action would count for nothing.

19 THE NEXT DAY, MCCARTHY SENT FOR JONATHAN Schell and myself to come to his suite. Schell was a grad student from Harvard who had been to Vietnam and written two short books about the destruction there. In Wisconsin he'd supplied a few detailed speeches about Vietnam, which McCarthy read out woodenly at banquets and never came back to. Goodwin had told McCarthy he would probably leave, and at his suggestion, McCarthy asked Schell and me to be his regular speechwriters, to "travel on the plane" with him for the rest of the campaign.

Flattered, we immediately agreed.

He leaned toward us confidentally, imposing in his heavy suit and heavy handsome face. His steel eyes had a hard blue twinkle. Around him a court had been assembled—staff, old friends, a chosen few of the press. He'd decided to be amused with us.

"It's narrowed down to Bobby and me," McCarthy said. "So far he's run with the ghost of his brother. Now we're going to make him run against it. It's purely Greek: he either has to kill him or be killed by him. We'll make him run against Jack. . . . And I'm Jack."

The eye on us was hard; you could not see in. I frowned uncertainly. McCarthy leaned back and laughed at us. For the others watching.

"Did you understand that?" Schell said outside the room.

"Half," I said. It was fascinating stuff for a politician.

"Well, I didn't."

Schell went back to Cambridge, unable to work against Robert Kennedy. I went to think about what McCarthy had said. I still got only half, and there wasn't any more, then or later.

20 A WEEK LATER, FLYING OVER NORTHERN INDIANA, I asked McCarthy to go over a speech with me. He sketched in rapid changes with a felt pen, faster than any editor I had seen. Like lightning he shucked away all that was unessential (even some good things), leaving natural elisions—which takes extraordinary intelligence and feel for words. Sometimes he did it indifferently, and the results were patchy, leaving nothing to say. But this time it went well, I learned something about writing speeches. It was easy enough to be humble about my newness to the trade, knowing as I did that a pure fluke had put me where I was, myself and others like me, that no ordinary Presidential campaign would take on a fiction writer over twenty years younger than the candidate with no time in service and no allegiance to his party.

McCarthy responded to humility. He stayed and talked for an hour about baseball. It was tough looking back into those slate-stone eyes which bore down hard and granted you nothing. Mostly he did not reply unless you played his straight man, feeding him lines. Half his remarks came weighted with a honking "Hunh?"—like a blow on the end of his flat strong farmer's voice. Impossible to answer anything but yes.

We proceeded with long intervals of silence. It turned out both of us had played first base. He reminisced with me—I wanted to stay with him. I began to talk about those moments of pure being—connecting with the ball, stabbing it from the air—coming through. Or the anguish of missing, the sensation of something gone so quickly you couldn't believe it wasn't still there.

No registration. After all, baseball doesn't matter. He probably knew that even as a player. I knew it only at times. And besides, it does matter.

McCarthy was nostalgic about the symmetry of the game, the perfect proportions. "I don't know how they put the pitching mound just where they did, *hunh?* But they found the perfect place."

He told me he didn't go to the Three-I League because he couldn't hit the curve ball. I was aware of his thick wrists, heavy hands, heavy bones: enormous power if he did make contact.

Later I saw a picture of him in the paper at batting practice, taking a tremendous stride into the ball. He could have hit a fast ball out of sight with those heavy bones and that stride. But I told him with a smile that a stride that long makes the curve ball unhittable.

"Hunh?" he said. "That's not my regular stride."

21 MARTIN LUTHER KING WAS ASSASSINATED BETWEEN the Wisconsin and Indiana primaries. The nation was treated to a TV parade of heavy government faces more concerned with cooling it than expressing their grief or—heaven forbid—their indignation. McCarthy was silent, preferring to keep his feelings unpolitical.

I remember flying into Washington, seeing pillars of smoke rising from the city. Angry soldiers grabbed you if you tried to go into the streets after dark.

The McCarthy campaign was in disarray. The men who occupied key positions on the national staff were nervous because there was no campaign strategy. There were non-meetings with McCarthy, where he would nod his head and say nothing to every specific proposal. Finally he would say that we would go on pretty much as before, but how was that? There were things to do, decisions to be made about the use of people and resources, a movement to be kept in motion; but in the absence of a form for making decisions, in the absence of a chain of authority, McCarthy's colonels and captains (some of whom had assembled the beginnings of the army) simply were not free to take initiative. Those who did were undercut, then or later. So day by day they wasted their energy in anxiety about their roles. The candidate's indifference was a rock on which they scraped: every day each left some remnant of his self-respect clinging there.

Goodwin had tried in his own way to hold things together,

but he was leaving now. After ten days of indecision and mysterious phone calls, it seemed his first loyalty, as he had known all along, must be to his friend. Yet Goodwin was hypnotized by McCarthy's potential as a candidate. He speculated that McCarthy might have been an ineffective candidate in 1960, when the country needed to be roused, but he could be a good one now, when the needs were dignity, honesty, and healing. Goodwin was tearing himself away from power, and he left telling McCarthy he was the front-runner now. Kennedy's intensity, he thought, would antagonize too many voters.

With or without McCarthy, our meetings got nowhere. With nothing else to do I passed the time writing campaign leaflets. One morning I wandered from the hotel and took a walk through the burnt-out part of Washington. Some of the bigger buildings were reduced to rubble—as though they'd been hit by blockbusters. In the side streets stood half-pretty little frame houses set on their own lots, run-down but perceptibly nicer than the tenements of New York. Most of the burning had taken place in the retail stores along the main streets of the ghetto. Now the black people who used to work in those stores stood aimless in the streets. As in the past, black anger had burned mostly against the physical surroundings of black people.

For all the talk about "revolution," the government part of Washington lay untouched. White block buildings sat unguarded behind stone fences on their plots of groomed green grass. If the riots had matched the rhetoric of certain rioters, a few commandos could easily have tossed grenades into the ice-like whiteness. On Saturdays and Sundays, they might have done it and walked away. But the riots came from anger and frustration, only the publicity came from ideology —so far.

While new fires burned the little stores of yet another ghetto, well-dressed white tourists strolled under the brilliant cherry blossoms along the Potomac basin. Here and there one saw an integrated couple picking their way along the sidewalk where elderly Negroes stood fishing.

At the foot of Washington's Civil War Memorial—a looming statue of General Sherman—a plump little beautiful brown boy is having his picture taken. His father stoops and twists to get Sherman in the frame, while his mother hollers, "Close your ugly little mouth!" The boy stands frozen in a gaping grin, paralyzed in his Sunday best, as his mother half-collapses in crazy embarrassed laughter and a column of smoke jumps up in the sky behind them.

22 THE YOUNGER PEOPLE WHO HAD REMAINED IN THE campaign were going through a perpetual identity crisis. At two in the morning my hotel room would fill with lost souls who had slaved all day but who weren't sure if they were really wanted or if they had any business being there. And we talked constantly about Bobby Kennedy: despite all the little cracks that were so easily justified, there was no final and conclusive reason for working against him.

The difference between the candidates was reflected in a polarization of the students who worked for them. Most of the Kennedy kids reminded me of the once-born boys and girls who serve on student councils and social committees. Loyalty for them was automatic, and they followed a leader rather than a cause. When we got to Oregon they used to spot me in the lobby of the Congress Hotel, and holler, "Jeremy, hey Jeremy, don't you wish you had a candidate who could *win*?"

The best of the McCarthy kids were the kind who wrote long papers all alone and got them in late because they were dissatisfied. Winning was a thrill but it unstrung them; it called into question their worry about being right and good. And for that very reason they worried all the harder about what Gene McCarthy and Robert Kennedy were doing to each other. Their work was more than conscientious; it was a compulsive act to quell the doubts that came the moment work left off.

The disposition of many of the McCarthy activists was to sit out the McCarthy-Kennedy primaries, but every time Bobby swung into action, he kept them working for McCarthy. A superficial Kennedy mistake was to offer high salaries for the canvassing work McCarthy paid for in peanut-butter sandwiches. When special Kennedy busses were sent off to campuses, McCarthy kids felt justified in riding them to Indianapolis, then walking around the corner from Bobby's headquarters in the Indiana Theater to McCarthy's in the Claypool Hotel. Poverty was a dearly assumed virtue for our young affluents, and it grew easier to talk of Bobby—in public—as if he really were the little rich kid pilloried on the front page of the *Indianapolis Star* for "trying to buy Indiana."

But there were more basic things that Bobby did that had "old politics" written all over them, beginning with his refusal to debate McCarthy. There was his flying visit to the

White House the moment Johnson dropped. There were the hacks who worked for him—Salinger, O'Brien, Sorensen, John Bartlow Martin, etc. The endorsement from McNamara which was a featured Kennedy TV ad. The harping on McCarthy's suggestion of a guaranteed income—which the McCarthy kids, as good students, knew was probably going to be necessary in some form or other. The stress on "law and order," which the kids took as an appeal to white racism; for example, the ads which announced that law-enforcement officers all over America endorsed RFK—and then listed a collection of people most of whom had once worked for the Justice Department.

The gimmick that backfired most loudly was the partisan attack on McCarthy's voting record which appeared in college papers in Indiana and on the West Coast. The ad was sponsored by the "Citizens for Kennedy" group which Kennedy soon repudiated; but student editors reported that the ads were arranged for by Pierre Salinger, and we also learned that in many localities the same material was distributed by Kennedy campaign headquarters. The general technique was to isolate one vote from McCarthy's record and pretend it represented his general position. For example, he had once voted against legislation of Ted Kennedy's to abolish the poll tax—but McCarthy explained that he did this on the advice of Attorney General Katzenbach, who did not want new legislation to complicate the upcoming hearing by the Supreme Court that soon resulted in the tax being declared unconstitutional. On all other occasions, McCarthy had voted against the poll tax.

When he first heard of the attack on his record, McCarthy said that it showed Kennedy was "unfit to be President." As late as December 1968—after all that had happened—he told the *Boston Globe* that it was his "greatest disappointment" of the campaign. But for serious young people, the kind Kennedy so ardently admired and desired, the attack turned out to be a plus for McCarthy.

Kennedy's generous admiration of McCarthy's youth brigade underscores the heavy irony of their daily disappointment with him—an irony that was anchored by the hidden iceberg qualities of our own candidate. The Kennedy slickness all of us knew too well—for example, the dubious aspects of his record as Attorney General. By personality and by history, Bobby's weaknesses were out in the open. The uncertainty, for example, the searching for identity, the impulsiveness, the seeking of meaning through action: all of this was paralleled in our own personal histories, where the privileges of affluence and education called alternately to action and despair, to public commitment and private elitism. We, too, were tempted, in our own way, by the prospect of taking the country into our own hands; and we were appalled at the symptom of our temptation writ large over Kennedy and the men who surrounded him—the blitheness, the lightning speed with which ends justified means.

Our own candidate had no past for us; he existed only in the present which we had helped to make. His oblique and scholarly idiom could not have been contrived; it left us free to assume that in his privacy and hesitation he embodied our more virtuous inner voices: those that sang of the true path and warned against corruption.

The division corresponded well to the temperamental opposition of the candidates. Bobby's inclination was activity: once he thought of something, he had to do it. McCarthy lay low: until proved otherwise, any given act was probably not worth the trouble. Bobby's characteristic sins were sins of commission; McCarthy's, sins of omission. It seemed that Bobby would tell people what to do—infringe on them, as he had with wiretapping—or get us involved in places we shouldn't be, as Rusk, McNamara, and other Kennedy appointees had done in Vietnam. McCarthy would "liberate" the population—leave us free to act in good faith—keep us from imposing our will on others. The clincher was the one exception to the rule. When it mattered, McCarthy had gone into New Hampshire. Bobby, hung up, had refrained.

Thus we criticized Kennedy's heavy-handed politicking; but we didn't know then that for McCarthy "new politics" meant little more than his personal freedom from commitments to anyone. We sneered at Kennedy's hacks—but we didn't know that McCarthy was getting some financial support from friends of Hubert Humphrey. As for "guaranteed income," McCarthy said those words twice—on March 19 at Howard University and on April 11 in Boston. The rest of the time he hedged with "a variety of programs to provide an assured income"—none of them spelled out. To his everlasting credit our candidate never mentioned "law and order" —but unlike Kennedy, he never addressed himself to the hatred and violence that made law and order an issue.

The ads on McCarthy's record were a smear, yes, because they failed to indicate the generally liberal pattern of McCarthy's congressional career. But in our smugness in recognizing dubious tactics, in our pleasure with the purity of McCarthy's positions, in our identification with his absolute righteousness, we McCarthyites, young and old alike preening ourselves on our intelligence and our moral alertness, didn't even bother to check the record. If we had, we might have learned what I have already indicated about McCarthy's careful attitude toward social change. He was for New Deal liberal aid programs, civil rights and civil liberties, but never for anything that challenged interests, rocked the boat, or threatened institutional reform. He was comfortable with the orderly processes of Congress and its committee structure, and there were many places where his liberal record reflected that comfort.*

On ethics and Senate procedures, for example, McCarthy had voted against every effort to pass a Senate income disclosure bill. In 1962 McCarthy voted in the Finance Committee and on the floor to let business lobbyists take their expenses as tax deductions. In 1967 he voted against an amendment by Senator Clark of Pennsylvania which would have prohibited joint business ventures by Senators and lobbyists. In 1966 McCarthy said the Senate Ethics Committee should not look into Senator Thomas Dodd's use of tax-free campaign funds—the grounds on which the Senate ultimately censured Dodd. During the following year McCarthy, as a member of the Ethics Committee, helped block an all-out inquiry into Dodd's financial dealings.

Although McCarthy was a critic of the unchecked power of the military and an advocate of change in America's priorities, he did not join the battle to reduce military appropriations. In 1964 he voted against two amendments reducing defense spending; in 1965 he voted or was announced against two more. In 1966 he voted against George McGovern's attempt to cut military aid funds by $250 million,

*For material on McCarthy's record, I am indebted to Robert Yoakum, a former Washington reporter.

though he did vote with the majority for a $100 million cut. On arms-related issues, in 1961 McCarthy voted for Barry Goldwater's amendment to prohibit the Arms Control and Disarmament Agency from conducting research. In 1967 he voted against Ted Kennedy's effort to cut a rifle-practice subsidy to the National Rifle Association from $428,000 to $200,000.

McCarthy's explanation for many of these votes rests on his regard for proper Senate procedures. For example, in explanation of a 1962 vote against reducing tax credit for gas pipeline investment, McCarthy said, "The floor shouldn't be cluttered up with irrelevant bills that haven't been worked out properly, or are brought up in the wrong way." Yet on December 25, 1966, he participated along with other Finance Committee members in loading the Foreign Investor Act with riders for the benefit of special interests. The Act became known as "The Christmas Tree Bill." George Lardner, Jr. commented in the *Washington Post*: "It didn't just happen. It was planned that way. It is a vivid example of how special interests influence the legislative process."

McCarthy not only voted for the riders put on by his associates, he contributed a beauty of his own, the "swap fund" amendment, which permitted stockholders to swap securities for shares in an investment fund without paying capital gains tax. Senator Williams of Delaware in opposing the amendment quoted treasury officials who said that it would "open a glaring loophole in the tax laws," for the benefit of "only seven or eight operations in America."*

Most of us simply could not imagine a man of strong

*Officers of investment funds were among the largest donors to McCarthy's 1968 campaign. Howard Stein of the Dreyfus Fund was National Finance Chairman.

liberal principles who did not connect them to institutional reform. We would never have guessed, for example, that although McCarthy, as a Congressman, courageously debated the notorious Senator Joseph McCarthy, he voted for every appropriation to the House Un-American Activities Committee, and voted to uphold every one of their contempt citations. In 1967 Senator Eugene McCarthy voted or declared against roll calls aimed at abolishing the Subversive Activities Control Board—and voted in favor of a bill continuing the Board.

Given his willingness to balance interests rather than challenge them, it is hardly surprising that McCarthy was not a crusader when it came to consumer practices or tax reform. Nor did it cut much ice with McCarthy people when Robert Kennedy raised these issues in his campaign. Nor did anyone but his speechwriters seem to notice McCarthy's glaring omission of Congressional reform in his references to a new politics. If we had bothered with the record, we would have known that in 1967 McCarthy joined seven Southerners in voting against the Legislative Reorganization Act, which drew a Democratic vote of 46 to 8.

We didn't look into these things because we didn't trust the Kennedys; the very style of the voting attack signaled to us that it must be a total smear. Then, too, there was McCarthy's utter righteousness and indignation, of a quality so massive and wrathful that it had to be sincere. Secularists that we were, we did not understand how philosophic and moral uprightness could be combined with contempt for piecemeal reform and personal involvement. Which is to say, we could not imagine the mind of Gene McCarthy.

And we needed so badly to believe that the loftiness of that mind encompassed and surpassed the frantic concerns of people like Kennedy and ourselves, whose causes and commitments could never entirely be separated from guilt or from ego satisfaction.

We acted, during the daytime, as if we were in the service of a wise and calm daddy, crudely attacked by a renegade brother who stirred up crowds with his long hair, squeaky baby talk, and unfair money. It helped that McCarthy had gone further on the big issues—especially the one overriding one—and he was the only candidate who was unconnected, we thought, with the Democratic machine. Our doubts focused on his willingness, his energy, his effectiveness. But there was, finally, in McCarthy's reserve, in all he left unsaid, a special air of mystery, a hint that he drew strength from a source beyond mere mortals like Kennedy and ourselves, a gift for grace that would tell him when and how to bring that strength to bear.

In Indiana one of McCarthy's young aides was approached very strongly by friends who worked for Kennedy. Night after night he agonized: there was nothing conclusive. But in the end he stayed and suffered. The reason finally was the one thing Kennedy couldn't offer:

"I thought McCarthy had a secret. I thought one day the secret would explain it all."

23

THERE NEVER WAS A MCCARTHY CAMPAIGN IN INDIANA and Nebraska. Our candidate went on giving his stump speech, and giving it well, but he did not react to the changing political climate, and in particular to the fact that he was no longer running against Lyndon Johnson and the war.

Indiana is the state where I grew up; wherever we went I talked to dozens of people. They had strong feelings about Bobby Kennedy; it was amazing how many would tell you they hated him. Roger Branigin had been inept as a governor, and most of the voters I talked to thought little of him—but they might vote for him to vote against Kennedy. McCarthy's problem was to establish himself as the alternative to Kennedy; otherwise, he would be regarded as merely a paler version of dovish liberalism. Given the provincial nature of Indiana and its rectionary press, most of the voters knew little about McCarthy when he came to their state from Wisconsin. After he had campaigned there for the better part of three weeks, they knew no more than before.

McCarthy might have done well in Indiana and Nebraska for the same reason he did well in the suburbs and rural areas of Wisconsin. Without Johnson and Vietnam, however, there was no ready-made backdrop to throw into relief his qualities of thoughtfulness, caution, and responsibility. The time had come to identify himself with a positive vision of America. McCarthy had such a vision, but he was content to go on expressing it in underdeveloped generalizations. "Details" remained anathema, and never did he stoop to exhort or persuade.

The news about McCarthy soon focused on the only points where he was specific: his sharply negative comments about marginal figures and issues. It seemed a matter of honor for McCarthy to insist on such comments even though they were peripheral to the major issues of the campaign. Time and again he would call for the firing of J. Edgar Hoover without any effort to enlighten his Midwestern listeners as to the abuses of the FBI or their relation to America's problems. A comment by advisers would redouble such references. Then one night a TV reporter asked McCarthy about the *Pueblo*, and he felt obliged to say he would ransom it—a statement that shocked Midwesterners and took up all the newspaper space devoted to McCarthy next morning.

At Indiana University, McCarthy drew good applause in a speech where he named the names that only he dared name. It was satisfying to be connected with the one candidate who could speak so frankly about the abuse of American power. But I was amazed afterwards to discover that many of the kids had left confused. "I just don't know what he stands for," said a girl in a Peter Pan blouse. "I don't know what he wants to do."

The arch-reactionary *Indianapolis Star*, the most powerful paper in the state, did not help with its incredibly slanted coverage. The front page of the *Star* was usually divided between Kennedy and Branigin, with an editorial cartoon in the middle of the top of the page depicting Bobby as a buck-toothed boy in shorts waving a wad of money. A few days before the primary, the major headline of the *Star* announced "Branigin May Be V.P." On May 6, the day before the election, the first page featured a large photo of Governor Branigin and two stories about him: nothing on Kennedy or McCarthy. In the *Star*, the issue was Eastern money and arrogance vs. Hoosier integrity. And that left McCarthy nowhere.

McCarthy could have used good advice, if he could have taken it, but since the departure of Goodwin he had isolated himself from professionals, and from the beginning he had no interest in those who approached him in terms of their commitment to the issues. His only companions were hangers-on and specially sympathetic journalists who toadied to McCarthy and took precious pleasure in the atmosphere of contempt toward politics and politicians. The Dump Johnson people were out of favor now that Johnson had been dumped; and indeed their canvassing operation had lost some of its better people and ran less effectively from Indiana on.

Among the loyal entourage were the Minnesota agency people, whose major concern was to ward off competitors from New York originally brought in by Goodwin (and later, in California, by Tom Finney). It was decided to divide TV time between spots made by both: the Minnesota were kind of homey, the New York spots had more content, and both were rather stiff. Nonetheless the array of spots would have presented McCarthy on a variety of issues—except that all but two of them mysteriously disappeared from the TV studios before they could be distributed. A New York spot of McCarthy on "reconciliation" ran again and again to the voters of Indiana. The New York people were fired—it was even whispered that the turncoat Goodwin had masterminded the plot. But soon afterwards I learned what happened to four excellent radio spots beautifully recorded by Paul Newman. One went on the air; the tapes of the others sat in the hotel room of the Minnesota agency man. It was not the last time in the campaign that films and tapes made by Johnny-come-latelies simply disappeared.

Over the years McCarthy had gathered a Senate staff who had more interest in their personal sinecures than in political issues; for his Senate office was hardly a center of feverish activity. Before 1968, these people had their very own Senator to care for; they tended the altar of his unappreciated brilliance and sensitivity. Now their man was threatened by a group of young know-it-alls, including all too many New York Jews (or "See-mites," as some of the real folk in McCarthy's office called them) who wanted to make him President.

Their clear duty, as they saw it, was to form ranks about the body and protect it from any disturbance not in accord with his own serene plan, which they believed in absolutely. McCarthy's personal secretary and his valet could be vicious to campaign staff who had business with him. On telephone calls they would hold the phone and sneer out the name of the caller, hoping for a savage insult they could repeat. Since sooner or later McCarthy put down everyone, these people held a certain political power: they could legitimately tell almost anyone that McCarthy had said he did not want to see him—or worse. Once John Gilligan, who was running for Senator from Ohio and who had influence among that state's delegation, tried to get to McCarthy in a Cleveland hotel. He was rebuffed both at the door and on the house phone; finally, he was permitted the honor of riding in an elevator with the candidate who was supposedly seeking his support.

McCarthy's valet was a tough little baby-faced law student who had worked in the Senate office operating the Xerox machine. At first in New Hampshire McCarthy was escorted by young political types, who tried to push him against his nature into the kind of handshaking activity that might have looked silly if the crowds had retained their original sparseness. So the valet was quickly installed by his side, and clung there like a weasel throughout the campaign. On occasion he would pull McCarthy back into his car as a friendly crowd of black people or Mexican-Americans moved to greet him. It was easy enough for advance men and campaign staff to blame him, but we soon found that he was earnestly striving to make himself an extension of his master's mood. One could measure one's daily standing with McCarthy by the degree of politeness or condescension one got from his valet.

Even more disturbing than his Senate staff was McCarthy's tendency to single out those campaign people who shared the propensity to grovel. Two of his favorites were a Harvard boy and his girl who came to believe they were a cut above the politically oriented canvassers. Soon they learned to hang on McCarthy's words and to guffaw loudly at his putdowns. Eventually he let them take charge of his press relations. They signaled their personal access by telling other people they were too excited, they should take it easy—the trademark of every dedicated McCarthy parasite.

The point is that none of McCarthy's flunkies was anywhere near him in intellect or talent. Their presence as well as his own attitude made it impermissible for anyone to engage him in open dialogue.

24 EVERYONE IN A POLITICAL CAMPAIGN IS REALLY ON A campaign all his own, striving to connect himself with other people in a way that will give him some satisfying congruence of who he is and what he does. Political people are hooked on contact. Usually they cannot do things all by themselves; they need to join with others if they are to have any sense of achievement. The lapse in McCarthy's campaign left too many who were busy and happy in Wisconsin

stranded in the Marrott Hotel on the near North Side of Indianapolis, an oasis of dullness at the end of a strip of girlie bars and cocktail lounges. Aides, ad men, schedulers, escorts, backers, hangers-on: they sit in the downstairs restaurant until the hostile Hoosiers close the kitchen at nine o'clock. Then they move to the bar. The reporters, too, are doing too much sitting, eating, drinking. Each one corners his favorite little boy or girl to find out what is really happening.

McCarthy himself eats sparingly in his suite on the seventh floor, has a few drinks and goes to bed early. He is offended at the excess food and drink, the spoilage, the waste. But it is needed, needed badly, for all these people to be worthy of filling themselves when there is nothing to do.

In a corner of the bar, the Administrative Assistant from McCarthy's Senate staff sits muttering and drinking. His role is to know the futility of it all. He is the Greek chorus of the campaign. He could hardly accept the new politics mystique. "I want to know who's getting poked. That's where the delegates are. No two campaigns are different. You hear that, Larner? The candidate will win despite the people working for him."

Can't stop talking about McCarthy. Been with him back in Minnesota, and off and on for twenty years, just as tall and just as bitter, reading the same poets and putting down the same phonies. Everyone in Washington is a phoney, if you only knew. Except the man upstairs.

"He's never lied to himself. He must know he's blown the last eight days. He knows because I told him. That's what you don't understand. He knows what he has to know. If you bug him you won't get a thing from him. He switches off after two words because he knows what the next half-hour is going to be. He can't stand anybody for half an hour. He's preoccupied. That's the political mentality, hunh? The big ones are all that way. Jack Kennedy was like that. McCarthy never says no to anyone. He never tells anyone what to do. But he's never made a mistake in his political judgment. Never made a mistake, and he never lies to himself."

Then there is the telephone disease, which in politics reaches epidemic proportions. You must be doing something if you are able to call someone, and you and he can tell each other who you are. There are all kinds of things to arrange that really do take phone calls. If you are anyone who matters you will have a direct line or two in your hotel room. You not only can, you must find out what's happening in other parts of the country, who is saying what, doing what, scheming what. The phone bill in Indiana runs $77,000.

The temptation is very great for the young people Curt Gans has put on his national staff. Most of them work hard all day in a kind of limbo. Indiana is a tough case, they have little contact with the candidate, hard to tell just what their efforts achieve, but by simply picking up the phone they can confirm their places in a national operation, collecting intelligence and planning plans all over the U.S.A. Often they will find it is important to fly somewhere, and they will have to rent a car when they get there. Then they will have to make more calls to report back to the people they are loyal to.

There is at last the moment when the *anomic* is too much to be fended off by food and drink and talk and phones, and the individual either disappears and goes back home or works himself into a religious frenzy wherein the gods are taking care of everything. He begins to sing and shout, to speak in tongues, to testify before the congregation.

On election day in Indiana, a little McCarthy aide goes scampering down the corridor.

"It hit me today!" he cries. "The feeling hit me!"

"It hit me yesterday!" yells the latest press secretary.

They grasp forearms and do a little dance grinning into each other's faces. McCarthy magic! Indiana is going to swing!

They touch off a small swirl of ecstasy. Lost souls hug and kiss cheeks in the corridor.

And who should come by but the man himself, with entourage piling up behind him.

The little aide grins up cutely right into the main face.

"I've got vibrations, Senator!"

"You feel it, hunh?" The face is worn, flesh-burdened, expressionless.

"Something hit the hotel this afternoon!"

The aide gets a pat on the back. All aroused, he tries to follow the entourage into the candidate's suite. But the valet turns just inside the door. "No," the valet says.

25 THAT NIGHT MCCARTHY NOT ONLY LOSES TO KENNEDY, but runs third behind Governor Branigin. He comes down the carpet to the elevator with his face dead and gray, twenty people crowding in silently behind him to go down in the same trip.

He is driven downtown to the old Claypool, no longer a hotel because the upper floors are condemned. There a miraculous event takes place. A few thousand canvassers are in from the storefronts, in from the precincts where they boarded with strangers and worked all night and day. The students stand now and cheer him and they cheer him and they cheer him. They are radiant with pride in themselves and all they stand for. Standing shapeless on the platform under the piercing arc lights, McCarthy begins to take on color; his jaw comes up, you can see him come alive. He tells them Indiana was like the pursuit race in Alice in Wonderland—everyone has won, though he doesn't know if everyone will get a prize. But they will go on.

And they cheer him for that. Letting him know that they are with him win or lose, just as proud, just as right, just as good.

It really is moving. There is a purity to it that is moving. There is something better and you want to think it has got to be.

Except on the box that night I had seen the violence at Columbia. TV tidbits for Mr. and Mrs. America, along with the evening body count from Vietnam. Kids bleeding from the clubs of bitter cops. Twisted screaming faces of the newly righteous. Simplicities of hatred, familiar people suddenly strange. Pushing, pushing on the country; refusing to be private, refusing to be kept. And here in the Hoosier heartland, in the slowness and meanness and lostness of my old home town, thousands of sweet young beauties cheering defeat as if it were a personal triumph.

Across at Kennedy's Sheraton-Lincoln it is seamy. Crowds of twitchy celebrity hunters in the lobby, manic, like *Day of the Locust*. Upstairs, middle-aged politicians wander the halls with dead cigar-stumps in their mouths like Lee J. Cobb. Blousy ladies' auxiliary ladies. Ethnic people looking ethnic, chosen and paid specimens of each variety, looking tough and soiled and ready to deal. Into the elevator floats a clutch of silken society plimps, tanned heads held at elegant angles, laughing vacant laughter into one another's mouths. Downstairs again the masses are restless. Where is he? Where is he? Each rumor twitches off a stampede.

In victory here there was only winning. Upstairs the soldiers came to divide up the spoils; downstairs, in the ballroom, bread and circuses. It was nobler across the street. But maybe, I thought, this ugliness is the center pit of America, this is what you win when you win it. When the marching and the cheering are done, this remains, this is what you have to deal with.

26 WHILE McCARTHY WAS IN NEBRASKA, I SPENT A FEW days in Los Angeles trying to straighten out some radio and pamphlet material. Something unpleasant had happened at the Los Angeles headquarters. The California campaign had been opened by enthusiastic amateurs, who got McCarthy on the top of the ballot by collecting 33,000 signatures between midnight and five a.m. on the first day of filing. As in Wisconsin, these people represented a wide range of talents. But key organizational posts had been captured by ambitious mediocrities who were guarding their own stations—and before long they had driven away many of the brightest and most idealistic volunteers.

The situation was repeated on the national level. In too many states the national staff drove out local talent—a typical campaign problem which happened in the Kennedy camp as well. But it was particularly disappointing that after the surge of high-spirited improvisation in New Hampshire and Wisconsin, the grass-roots campaign did not work in Indiana or Nebraska. Inexperience was telling in states that lacked a network of antiwar Democrats and in a campaign suddenly deprived of LBJ. Talent and experience were repelled by insecurity—and insecurity was deepened by a refusal of the candidate himself to seek out talent or to delegate authority. With no clear lines of responsibility, insecurity worked to bolster itself—as in many more ordinary campaigns. Luckily, the state of Oregon was better organized, due partly to a strong peace movement and partly to the fact that Susan Thomases administered an effective volunteer operation with a staff recruited largely from talent cast-off from the national staff after Wisconsin. No one who was important in Oregon had any status in the national organization either before or after the victory there.

A member of the McCarthy family once bitterly denounced the entire national staff to me, from campaign manager Blair Clark on down. Why then did McCarthy choose them, I asked. I was told that these were the people who came; he had chosen no one. It is sad to think of this: that after twenty years in national politics, Eugene McCarthy knew of no experienced organizers whom he could turn to, that even when he was running for President, he had no talented friends who would come to him. Part of the problem, as we have seen, was that the political allies he had made were not the kind of people who opposed the war.

Though there were some intelligent and dedicated people on the national staff, the most outstanding individuals were more comfortable near the bottom of the organization, where some of them ran brilliant operations in storefronts, far enough removed so that they could idealize the candidate and give full play to their own particular talents.

Many of them were anarchic idealists, who came into amusing conflict with the clever young operatives who were often sent to direct them. Once an urban expert prepared a leaflet sharply pointing up the discrepancies in Kennedy's various civil-rights positions. But the mimeograph crew at the L.A. headquarters thought it was unfair and refused to run it off. Their decision stuck.

One day in California, a young professional named Sandy Frucher who had been with the campaign from the beginning and had in fact opened the first McCarthy office in Washington, had the problem of dealing with squads of hecklers sent by the Kennedy people to block McCarthy. Seeing them form ranks outside a hotel where McCarthy was to emerge, Frucher quickly put on his Kennedy button and approached with authority. "McCarthy's coming out the side door!" he shouted. "We've got to head him off!" The hecklers rushed around the corner, McCarthy came out and left for Watts.

Frucher had to skip Watts to prepare a reception afterwards. He gave the button to his assistant and told him he would have to pull the same stunt later.

That afternoon Frucher waited while the candidate was inexplicably delayed an extra hour in Watts. Finally the caravan arrived, and Frucher's assistant explained that the hecklers had caught up with McCarthy, surrounded him and prevented him from going on.

"But didn't you use the button!" Frucher screamed.

The assistant sadly shook his head.

"Sandy," he said, "that's not our kind of campaign."

27 IN SAN FRANCISCO ON MAY 20, CAMERA CARRIAGES rolled like catapults across the ballroom of the Hilton Hotel; grips in shirtsleeves scuttled to set up blinding lights. It had been advertised that McCarthy and Kennedy would speak to Bay Area labor leaders who had gathered to eat for COPE under the glittering chandeliers. The Kennedy turned out to be Teddy, but still the dinner was the first public McCarthy-Kennedy encounter of the campaign.

Teddy led off, and we could see right away he was a speech-writer's dream. The whole thing, even the jokes, was delivered from script: and well delivered, earnestly, confidently, but not too expertly, so that you could tell the young actor really meant his lines.

The local McCarthy people had been talking up a cop-out by Bobby, but Teddy took that head-on (just as Bobby took "ruthlessness") with some generous jokes on Bobby and himself. From then on the audience was in his hand, and even sat still for a schoolboy's history of the American labor movement, going back to the Triangle Shirtwaist fire. Teddy's theme was that "labor never turned aside" from the great problems of the day—and that it would not turn now from Vietnam and the crisis of our cities. So he had a little pill for the fur coats and double breasts, and all the sugar-coating was to get it down. It was a good job, modestly done, and painless to the powers who now rose and applauded the Kennedy who had come to them.

We were afraid for McCarthy. He looked fifty years older, worn and bored by the whole routine. Perhaps he would decline to speak at all.

But he launched in hard, in a voice strong with irritation and pride, and gave one of his better offhand speeches. He talked about how he had worked for migrant workers when it was not a popular cause. He talked about how in 1959 he had tried to amend the Landrum-Griffin Act to allow unions to pay for the legal defense of their officers—and how his motion got only seven votes on the floor of the Senate. He improvised something new on his theme of new civil rights: how freedom of speech must now include "the right to have access to the truth," how the freedom of assembly must include "the right to organize"—and how the right of privacy now must include a defense against "electronic forms of prying." He didn't have to mention that another candidate had used such "subtle forms" against another labor leader.

McCarthy was coming on strong, he might have carried the day. But he concluded strangely, "This is a year in which some of us have talked about the need for a new kind of politics. I think that this may be to overstate it. It may be that what we need is old politics, the kind of politics we had in this country back in 1932 and 1936." A put-down for us, yet perhaps meaningful or reassuring to the labor people had he explained what he meant—but no, it turned out to be "a politics of reasoned judgment." McCarthy was settling for a draw, and as he asked for their support he ducked his head and trailed off.

28 McCARTHY HAD "POOR-MOUTHED" HIS BAD DEFEATS IN Indiana and Nebraska, refusing to congratulate Kennedy and speaking as if he had won some sort of moral victory. But he knew very well that he faced humiliation in California and elimination from the race if he could not pull out Oregon. Up against the wall, he demoted Curtis Gans and accepted a seasoned Democratic professional as campaign coordinator. Tom Finney was a partner in Clark Clifford's law firm, who had been at various times a CIA man, a White House aide under Johnson, and Adlai Stevenson's floor manager at the 1960 convention. Finney was experienced in what might be called "the politics of effectiveness" behind the scenes in Washington; that was why he had been active in the effort to get the Vice Presidency for McCarthy in 1964. He couldn't have cared less about "new politics," student canvassers, storefronts, or grass roots, but he was sincere in his opposition to the war and in his belief that it must be repudiated by the Democratic Party. Finney wanted to professionalize McCarthy's staff, streamline his schedule, and sharpen up his TV spots. He even insisted that the advance men were to guide McCarthy on tours, so that the valet could not pull him away from crowds.

The other speechwriter from Indiana through to the end was Paul Gorman, a 27-year-old who had done writing and research for a group of nine liberal Congressmen. Together Gorman and I decided that McCarthy would use full texts with programmatic content if we could imitate his style and adapt our arguments to the rhetorical framework of balanced government and reasoned judgment. Whether goaded by defeat or by Finney, McCarthy did indeed begin to give speeches that reporters could report, and relied on texts for major statements on the West Coast and on numerous occasions from then on. At Corvallis on the first day in Oregon, he used a text on the military-industrial complex in which he detailed facts and figures and called for reconversion programs, cuts in the defense budget, limits on the military influence in universities, curtailment of arms sales, and removal of the military from foreign-aid programs. In San Francisco the next night he traced the history of the assumptions and decisions that led to disaster in Vietnam. In a speech that week at the University of California at Davis, he set forth a complete urban program, winding up with a proposal for "new towns" to "bring workers where the jobs are."

It was a political necessity at this point for McCarthy to dramatize his differences with Robert Kennedy, but we were surprised to see the pleasure he took in deriding Bobby and the power with which he began to play with his audience. Some of his attacks were legitimately scornful of Kennedy's "old politics" techniques. But the mockery began to take on a disturbingly personal edge. He talked as though Bobby were a fake and nothing more. He developed a whole new bit ridiculing Bobby's dog Freckles. Audiences egged him on, either from hatred for Kennedy or from a guilty need to feel they were on the right side in a contest of good *vs.* evil.

It got out of hand the very first night in the question period at Corvallis, when McCarthy, after giving sharp strong answers to one question after another, casually remarked that the educated people were voting for him, and the less educated for Bobby. This was sure to be picked up by TV and by the Kennedy people.

I wanted to believe he did not mean it in the worst sense, and I brought it up afterwards as we rode to the airport.

"Was that unfair?" McCarthy said.

"I think it was," said Gorman quickly.

"But it's true," McCarthy said.

"What does that mean?"

"Nothing!" he laughed.

29 BUT IT WAS WORSE THE NEXT NIGHT IN THE COW Palace. The day before, as we flew from Klamath Falls to Coos Bay, a reporter from Metromedia had asked McCarthy a standard hypothetical question about whom he might support if he himself had no chance for the nomination: were there any circumstances in which it might be Humphrey?

"I don't know," McCarthy said into the man's tape recorder. "I think I'll wait and see what his position is on the war." He went on to say it was "not impossible" that Humphrey might change his position.

It went right out over the wires, and by the end of the day telephone calls were coming in to campaign headquarters not only in Oregon and California, but in New York and all over the country. The McCarthy movement absolutely would not stand for the man who had not only waved every bloody flag he could reach, but who had intimated that those who didn't were lacking in courage and patriotism. To them, Humphrey was the enemy, and they called in asking if McCarthy had really said it. If he had, they could no longer work for him. Unless he took it back, McCarthy's entire campaign was about to collapse around him.

By the end of the day McCarthy was saying that he had been misquoted. He was ready to set the matter straight in the Cow Palace the next night. "Will you attack Humphrey for his involvement in the war?" I asked him. "Attack him as hard as you attack Kennedy?" He said he would. If he had said no, I would have had to leave myself, and I would not have been the only one. We had not come that far for Hubert Humphrey.

When we got to Portland for the night, I phoned several advisers back East to see what they would say about Humphrey. Late that night I put together some language on our Vice President. He had not only supported the war, he had become "its most ardent apologist." "And those who sought, in the best American traditions, to question our policies, were subject all too often to his ridicule and scorn." And just to clinch it: there must be a distinction "between those who have objected to our present policies in Vietnam and those responsible for them."

Gorman in the early hours of the morning put the criticism into a context which was compatible with the best that McCarthy stood for. "Vietnam was no accident," it was the consequence of a series of misconceptions about America's role in the world. The containment policies of the Fifties had become "articles of faith," built into institutions which had assumed "unprecedented power," beyond any kind of political accountability. The policies were implemented by leaders who had emerged from "a sort of University of the Cold War"—and who had been guiding American foreign policy ever since.

In the Sixties, containment assumed the form of "counter-insurgency, a kind of containment from within." "We took upon ourselves the duty to judge the political systems of other nations and to alter those systems if we found them wanting." The rhetoric seemed new, but America was still acting as "world judge and world policeman." Thus when America began to move into Vietnam, "the folly of earlier years received its fullest expression—from the advocates of the Cold War: Dean Rusk, Walt Rostow, McGeorge Bundy, and William Bundy." (McCarthy scratched out here the one name Hubert Humphrey—perhaps fairly—up to 1965 there was little to choose between Humphrey and McCarthy on foreign policy.)

It was legitimate, then, to criticize Kennedy in this context as a man who, in the early Sixties, "played a prominent role in formulating policies which resulted in disastrous adventures." McCarthy could then say he was not sure Kennedy had "entirely renounced" the "systematic misconception" from which those policies sprang. "I have not heard him criticize the military in this nation, or the Department of State, or the CIA. He has been silent about Dean Rusk [and] Robert McNamara. . . . He continues to call upon America to assume . . . 'moral leadership on this planet'—an echo of John Foster Dulles" (and the final phrase of Kennedy's announcement of candidacy).

The text went on to Humphrey, who had become in the past three years "a new champion" of "the same assumptions, institutions, and leaders," and continued with the language I have already given. One conclusion could then cover both Kennedy and Humphrey: leaders of the future must be free from errors of the past, if the American people are to assure themselves that those errors will not be repeated.

There were questions the Cow Palace speech did not raise —important questions about the nature of modern Communism and its role in the underdeveloped world. In retrospect, it was a little too easy, a little too tuned to the times. But the speech defined a critical break with the mechanism of past policy: a standard by which Humphrey was hopeless and Kennedy problematical.

We hammered out language most of the way to San Francisco, getting out a final text as the plane settled on the runway. That night we went to the Cow Palace in trepidation. McCarthy had corrected the text carefully—it had already been released and would do the job of retaining the faithful. But the production of the text would be in itself an act of deception unless McCarthy actually spoke the words about Humphrey. Without the attack on Hubert, the language on Bobby would be out of proportion and unfair.

It took a while to get to the text. McCarthy reviewed his decision to run, pointing out that he had been willing to take chances—unlike "the Senator from New York" who was "concerned about his future." Then he swung into Kennedy in his favorite way, doing his bit on Freckles and stretching out the bit about the twenty-six varieties. Suddenly, a new low: "There was a story the other day that Senator Kennedy was sore—they said he was trying to avoid the image of his brother—but he didn't want to be himself."

The arena was dark—I think it was mostly filled with very young people. As they laughed it up, I felt a sickness in the pit of my stomach. Was this what it meant to be "purely Greek"?

But McCarthy was into the text, embellishing it in a way that gave it depth and richness, improvising relevant additions on the pressures of the China lobby. He gave the written criticisms of his rivals equal space, adding some sharpening phrases: ". . . nor is the Vice President prepared to say that the process is wrong as well as what it produces." Yet he swallowed the word "his" when he said that those who "sought . . . to question policies have been subject . . . to [his] ridicule and scorn"—so that the phrase lost its application to Humphrey. It was disturbing too that McCarthy delivered the sentences on Humphrey in a subdued, rapid tone. And when it came to the distinction between candidates for the war and against it, McCarthy said it in a garbled way that could not have made sense to his audience.

The next morning McCarthy was in the clear. The text had been printed in *The New York Times* and circulated to all campaign headquarters. He had officially put down Humphrey on a equal basis with Kennedy—and since the speech was very late at night, and on the West Coast, the reporters had had to go by the advance text, so that in the papers the criticism was exactly even.

Was it overscrupulous that we still worried about who McCarthy was and where he might eventually go? It was politically justifiable to invite a Humphrey vote against Kennedy in the primaries—still, it was now clear that McCarthy hated Bobby Kennedy, that on a personal level he preferred Humphrey. We hoped it was only personal. Even on that level, the tone of mockery was sometimes sickening —but wasn't it more important that the movement was going to continue, and that we were backing the only candidate who could deliver an indictment of the State Department and the military? Our efforts were shadowed now by the chance that they might go in the end to make a peace plank for Hubert Humphrey: but standing in the way of that was the near-unanimous resistance of our whole constituency—and the personal pride of Eugene McCarthy and Lyndon B. Johnson.

30 IN THE LITTLE TOWNS OF OREGON MCCARTHY WOULD lope down Main Street with his left hand in his coat pocket, shaking hands on his way to the local TV or radio station—and I would trail him on the other side of the street, pretending to be a reporter. "You're from New York, aren't you?" the people said to me. "Oh, he's a very independent man, I guess. I'd be for him as President. Either him or Reagan."

In the small-town headquarters I would be challenged by two or three lively housewives who had worked hard for McCarthy's visit to their county. They were all for him on the war. "But what does he say about gun control? We've got twenty-three rifles in the family, we're proud of the way our six-year-old can shoot. He's not going to take away our right to bear arms, is he?"

Rest assured, ladies. He wasn't.

NOBODY KNOWS

31 THERE WE WERE IN BEAUTIFUL EARLY SUMMER, touring two of the country's most liberal states with probably the two most politically advanced candidates ever to run at the same time, two men who were concerned with the issues and scornful of corn-pone appeals to motherhood and God, each out supposedly to inspire a new sense of urgency and hope in America. It should have been the peak of the campaign, yet the issues were personal, and the tone was always wrong. The campaign was doing bad things to the candidates, bad things to the people who worked for them, bad things even to the partisans who looked on from afar with contempt for one another.

On the Sunday morning before election day in Oregon I went in by private car to join our tour in a mountainside park above Portland. Driving in, I saw Kennedy's press bus sitting at the entrance to a little railway at the upper end of the park. Kennedy was choo-chooing high among the giant fir trees, and his caravan was waiting for him to descend. It occurred to me that here was a chance to produce the confrontation we had sought for weeks—to force Kennedy either to an exchange of views or a proof that he was ducking debate—one of the constant themes of our Oregon TV and radio spots.

I jumped out of the car and ran down to the lower end of the park, where McCarthy was strolling through the rose garden like the Queen of Hearts, followed by staff, press, and a crowd of eleven persons. "Kennedy's up there!" I shouted to

McCarthy's custodians, pointing toward the platform a quarter-mile uphill and thinking they would dig what's happening right away. But the deuce and the trey of hearts saw it as a chance to reinforce their role-playing and drawled just like their master that I should take it easy, don't get excited. Just the sight of him gets you in a lather, hey? Heh heh.

It took me five minutes to turn the procession and get it moving grandly up the incline. By this time the photographers were dashing up and down and prodding the party onward. My only worry was that Kennedy would get off his train, size up the scene, and split before we got there. Just then I ran into three students with virgin beards and McCarthy buttons.

"Run on ahead," I told them, "and stand in front of Kennedy's car!"

I turned back again to the royal party, but within a minute Kennedy had disembarked and gone for his convertible. I ran up the hill with the *Life* photographer just behind me, yearning for a shot that would beat out his Kennedy counterpart. When I got to Kennedy's convertible it was moving slowly forward. My three demonstrators were backing in front of it holding it off with their outstretched hands. If I had told them to lie down, we might have tested the "ruthless" image once and for all.

My charge carried me right up to Kennedy, who was sitting on top of the back seat with his brown and white spaniel next to him, just like in the photographs. Kennedy shrank a little, as if I were going to grab him. He was smaller than I thought, and his eyes were a brilliant blue.

Every second I could hold him talking would bring McCarthy that much closer into camera range.

"Senator McCarthy is coming," I grinned. "Why don't you stick around and have a talk with him?"

I was standing over him and he was looking at me with a look of exquisite hurt. Did we think he was running from fear?

"Isn't that too baaad!" he said.

He turned to his driver and the driver floored it, the kids jumped for their lives.

So Kennedy rolled down the hill without looking back, and I stood with the *Life* photographer shouting "Coward! Chicken!" —for truly, he was running away.

It turned out that we had held him just long enough for the TV crews to get McCarthy coming and Kennedy speeding off. That night all Oregon saw our backs, and heard the shouts of Coward. Followed by McCarthy capturing the Kennedy press bus and shaking hands with Kennedy's abandoned press.

For five minutes I felt exhilarated. It was a lot of fun, like winning a game of touch football. I didn't think about it till I saw the film on TV back at the hotel and heard the parasites joking in the corridors. When I heard my own voice pipe Coward, I got that flash of nausea that had come before in the Cow Palace.

I thought about Kennedy. Of course he wasn't surprised by the act itself. That wasn't what hurt him. He would have done the same himself, had done the same or worse many times and without hesitation.

But what was *I* doing then, I who had joined for a cause and worked to state the issues? I had acted from instinct —just like any other hack—to embarrass the opposition. I had become in my way pretty much like everyone else on either side: a gangster in a war of two mobs in the same family.

The hurt look was no cry for pity: it was the registration that something had gone terribly wrong in our fight for the territory. I could grin and play the game and he knew the tough answer, but our family could only lose, and what did I know, what did I really know, that made me so eager to beat him?

32 WE WON OREGON, KENNEDY MADE A GRACIOUS concession speech, and we hopped through sunny California, the airports, the campuses, the freeways and shopping centers. Everywhere we had bands and crowds of students who kept McCarthy happy. For one week he felt like a winner, smiled and saw America smile back at him. Those moments when he got off the plane and we heard the blues groups play "When the Saints Come Marching In" and saw the home-made signs and the very serious good people our serious crowd-pullers had pulled cheering with rapture: you could believe good things about this country and what was happening to it. The best sign of all said simply, "We Believe You."

Once in Huntington Beach McCarthy was driven right down on the sand and talked to a crowd of wildly dressed beachcombers—who listened carefully and responded with savvy. You just never knew who was listening and who they might be. We drove down the freeways with the kids in the caravan making V's at the people passing and sure enough getting more often than not two fingers in return. That simple sign was tremendously gratifying for them—as if they were altar boys of a secret society about to come forth and turn on the world. The new American Dream! At our night-time rallies the healthy young ones cheered with blood lust for McCarthy's ever more confident slams at Kennedy.

Truly, McCarthy was picking up in California. It looked as if he might win the state—and if he did he would be the leading contender for the nomination.

Of course not everyone loved us—it was clear the Mexicans and Negroes were going to go heavily for Kennedy. But that was all the more reason, some of us thought, for McCarthy to talk to them—as the leader of his movement and as a potential leader of this country. Norval Reece, our dedicated scheduler, and the workers who made arrangements, were constantly trying to get McCarthy to make as many ghetto appearances as possible.

McCarthy was "willing" if not eager, and he did go, but the spirit was not with him. Once we were flying into L.A., where we would make a quick stop in Watts before moving on to a TV studio. McCarthy would not make a speech, but we thought it would be helpful to release a statement of his views on jobs, welfare and other problems. On the plane I told the valet I had a statement to clear with McCarthy right away, or else there would not be time to have it mimeographed and passed out in Watts. "Are you kidding?" the valet said. "Those people can't read. They'll *eat* your press release!"

33

NEVERTHELESS IT WAS ON THE ISSUE OF RACE AND THE cities that McCarthy made an important distinction between Kennedy and himself. We had been wanting to give McCarthy a strong urban text to stem those critics who said he didn't care about the ghettos and had developed no program for them. Our thought was that on election day in Oregon he could deliver that text for his scheduled stop at the University of California at Davis: the headlines next morning might say McCarthy wins in Oregon and (lower down the page) McCarthy opens week in California with major urban program.

To me, McCarthy had two ideas about poverty and race which had the potential for basic social change: (1) that the society as a whole must make significant cash outlays in the fundamental areas of jobs, housing, health and education; (2) that poverty of minority groups stems from "isolation" or "colonialism," and must be remedied by integration. McCarthy himself, as I have shown, presented these commitments in terms of moral obligation rather than political or economic transformation. In the postwar years just before he came to Washington in 1948, the President and the Congress had promised America full housing, full employment, complete health services and public education. But these programs had been implemented by only token programs with token funding, and those who could have benefited from them had been brought to despair and violence. McCarthy had been saying that now we needed to fulfill our obligation, and he stressed the Kerner recommendation that we build six million new housing units in the next five years—a program in line, say, with federal highway spending. Beyond that, McCarthy stuck to the vagueness of "the four new civil rights." He was light on detail, but his general approach cut to the roots of the problem.

The McCarthy approach was completely unfashionable in the election campaign of 1968. The clichés of the year were that black separatism was "new and exciting," that "black capitalism" (Richard Nixon) and "community action" (Robert Kennedy) could "rebuild the ghetto" through "incentives to private industry." The stress on "free enterprise" was characteristic of every candidate but McCarthy. Humphrey's publicized "Marshall Plan for the Cities" was not only a hash of undeveloped, unrelated fragments, but its basic approach was through private incentives.* Robert Kennedy argued that the public approach hadn't worked, but he was more on the beam when he said that it couldn't be got through Congress. The American people were simply not ready to spend what it takes to create real change—that is why they were doomed to go on having riots. The truth was that public programs on an effective scale and coordinated with an over-all economic plan had never been tried. Private industry, on the other hand, had been given a good crack at the ghetto—and had shown a consistent ability to exploit cheap Negro labor and to appropriate the real estate on which black people lived.

1968 was a good year for black separatists to get Republican foundation grants, for black businessmen to get small loans, and for black militants to get their hands on the treasuries of pilot poverty programs. None of this interfered in the slightest with the functioning of the corporate structure, or gave the slightest inconvenience to white people in the suburbs. It offered a way of "solving the problem" without actually having to deal with black people. The only trouble

*Ironically there were those in the labor movement, including some socialists, who hailed Humphrey's commitment to public programs, and claimed that McCarthy had no urban program whatever. Cf. the writings and speeches of Penn Kemble and Brendan Sexton, the publications of the League for Industrial Democracy.

was that the problems of the ghetto remained, and the money reached very few of the people living there. "Black power" is easy to say, but the question is power over what? Southern small towns for years have let their "Nigras" run their own side of the tracks. The resources of a wealthy society remain safely in other hands.

Robert Kennedy's Bedford-Stuyvesant project has done good things for its community—and so have legitimate community action programs. But they cannot in themselves be nearly sufficient—and in fact the Kennedy experiment has lost ground without the presence of its famous originator.

If one combined the basic programs of the Kerner Report with the redesign of urban living arrangements—which are breaking down anyway—one would come up with a significant alteration of the situation that perpetuates the cycle of poverty and discrimination. We weren't sure it would be good politics—that would be up to McCarthy. But it would answer the need to spell out an urban program. And this was a Democratic primary, not a general election—surely there were liberals and Negroes who recognized the thinness of Kennedy's approach behind the genuine passion of his commitment. No one who was already going to vote for McCarthy would switch because he didn't copy the urban approach of Robert Kennedy—and some undecideds might be won over by a serious and positive program. The program would be in line with what McCarthy had been saying. And besides, it was right—I think.

Before writing the speech, I talked it over with Gorman and our researchers, and with Neil Gold, a young urbanist from New York who in the fall of 1967 had impressed McCarthy with the fact that although job opportunities declined steadily in core urban areas, there were a quarter of a million openings for unskilled workers in industry located in "the belt line" around our major cities. In a text released for an early campaign speech in Manchester, New Hampshire, on December 15, McCarthy had stated that "an effective solution to the problems of minority unemployment and to . . . family instability, poverty, segregation . . . must look toward the movement of large numbers of Negro workers and their families to jobs and housing opportunities in the nation's suburbs." When we talked in Oregon, Gold now suggested a means to expedite that goal: a program for building "new towns" from scratch on the outskirts of urban areas.

The Davis text began with the assertion that "the situation is getting not better but worse . . . for the people who live in the ghettos, where they are locked away from the affluence of American life, treated as a colonial people in the midst of a society that does not honor their claim to equality or participation. . . .

> By promising progress but failing to deliver it, the Administration has actually deepened the crisis it ought to have been resolving. The War on Poverty, minimal and misdirected to begin with, is a casualty of the war in Vietnam. Yet the Vice President speaks of a "politics of happiness," as though the young men of the ghetto should rejoice that the government has given them a few summer jobs to keep them off the streets.* By his failure to endorse the Riot Commission report, Vice President Humphrey has called into question his willingness and commitment to deal with the principal domestic problem of our time.

*Later in the campaign, the summer job funds were cut by about eight percent, which undercut Humphrey as well.

"Poverty in America is no accident, anymore than Vietnam is an accident"—a tie-up with the Cow Palace speech. Then down to the brass tacks of isolation.

> Since World War II, Negroes forced off the land in the rural South have come in increasing numbers to the central cities. Meanwhile white people have been leaving the cities for better homes and jobs in the suburbs. Eighty percent of the new jobs in metropolitan areas are outside the central cities. Most of these jobs do not require a college education. Yet poor people are locked in the middle of the city . . . .

Gilding the ghetto therefore has severe limitations.

> There is not enough land, there are too many people, and there simply will not be enough jobs and housing. . . . The crisis of the ghetto is bound up with the structure of our entire society. The ghetto will not be fundamentally affected until a new politics in America addresses itself to our society as a whole.

Then the criticism of Kennedy.

> That is why I am disappointed by Senator Kennedy's over-emphasis on rehabilitating the ghetto through private enterprise. . . . The ghetto may have a few more factories and a few more jobs, but it will remain a colony, it will retain its economic and political dependence. . . . Certainly apartheid offers no solution. Private programs designed solely to rehabilitate the ghetto leave open to question our commitment to an integrated society. Rehabilitation financed by a profit-making outside organization can easily become paternalism.

> The only way to reduce poverty is to attack it at its roots, to eliminate the conditions from which poverty springs.

There followed an outline of proposals for "An Open America," beginning with the basic programs for housing, jobs, education and health. Some of these programs were combined with new forms of "participation," for example: "The people who will live in these [new housing] units should be given the opportunity to build them." The "new towns" would provide "our most effective way of creating job-linked housing programs." They would offer greater possibilities of participation, since "residents will better be able to run their own schools and services, get together in town meetings to make the decisions which affect their lives."*

> New towns are more attractive to industry, since they offer low tax rates, easy access, and a pleasant environment in which to work. Industry could play a very positive social role, since integrated hiring practices would immediately produce integrated communities.

The Davis speech pointed out that "two-thirds of our people are packed into one percent of our land. . . . It is time to bring the workers where the jobs are"—both by housing and by mass transit from the center of the city.

> Eventually we are going to have new cities and towns in the United States. We would need them whether there were poor people or not. The question is whether or not we are going to plan them to relieve the congestion and blight of our cities.

*In "decisions which affect their lives" we had picked up what became *the* leading cliché of 1968.

McCarthy seemed happy with the text, especially with the criticism of Kennedy. He himself inserted the word "apartheid." He was stiff, however, in delivering the speech. I realized listening to him that the style was too direct and unphilosophical for his taste. He was adding the philosophy as he went along, putting in so many qualifiers and explanations that he got only halfway through. It was a hot day at Davis, and the rally was outdoors with an unshaded bandstand: really not a place to deliver a long serious speech.

Yet there may have been a more basic reason for our candidate's discomfort. The implications of his own premises, when spelled out in detail, were that something was wrong not merely with the balance but with the structure of certain American institutions. To overcome the effects of racism and urban decay would then require radical social dislocations. By temperament McCarthy did not press to that uncomfortable conclusion.

But the text was released, and immediately drew the fire of Kennedy's younger staff, who prided themselves in their identification with the ghetto and their realism about its problems. Since their kind of private enterprise was connected with the rhetoric of "black power," they considered their candidate to be both more radical and harder of nose.

34 ON JUNE 1 WE WENT UP TO SAN FRANCISCO FOR THE television debate that Kennedy had at last been forced into. For the day-to-day surveys showed that McCarthy was coming on strong among the California exurbanites. He was serious

and confident on all the little radio and TV interviews that Kennedy perhaps mistakenly passed up. The Kennedy people didn't seem to think their man was at his best on TV; at any rate they had him covering more ground than McCarthy and demonstrating again and again his ability to pull a huge, wild crowd. Not all of McCarthy's admirers were as fervent to touch him or see him in the flesh, but they were quietly impressed with a man whose star was rising from Oregon. He had been the first man to beat a Kennedy, and that Kennedy could no longer let it be said he was afraid to debate.

The Kennedy people had vetoed a direct debate, insisting on a panel asking questions, as in the Nixon-Kennedy debate of 1960.* Still the attitude of McCarthy's camp followers was one of lofty confidence. They knew their man was the more articulate speaker and a more soothing presence on TV. Only Finney and a few others were worried: we knew that Kennedy would be up against the wall and prepared to the teeth. He was slipping—he absolutely could not afford to lose or look smaller. And we knew there was no way of knowing how McCarthy might react to the situation: the motives he might have for trying or not trying, coming on or stepping back.

Gorman and I, along with Arthur Herzog, the McCarthy campaign manager in Oregon, and Tom Morgan, Stevenson's former campaign press secretary, prepared a briefing book

*It is pathetic that after millions of dollars are spent campaigning in America, spent on rallies and stunts and propaganda, neither the public nor the networks insist that the candidates directly engage one another on TV. In the Kennedy-McCarthy encounter, the panel acted mainly as an obstruction. The questions were fatuously put, with no glimmer of the polar differences between these candidates.

which consisted of all the questions that might be asked, plus Kennedy's anticipated replies, and suggested answers combining what McCarthy had said and what he might say if the going got rough. Actually we did anticipate most of Kennedy's subsequent attack. McCarthy carefully went over the briefing papers with Tom Finney—but when the debate started it was as if he had gone in cold.

And he was right, I think, to rely on his own instincts. He had been celebrated as a man who knew how to act in a moment of crisis. A debate is not a speech, and set pieces could never be as effective as a display of natural authority. To go in cold would be to take a risk—a risk of the sort that John Kennedy would never take against Nixon and Nixon would never take against anyone. But McCarthy was the man who was ready to take risks in 1968. If he really had the power we wanted to believe he had, he might sit back under pressure and drop his shots with all the timing and accuracy that should have been building in him over the months. The debate was a test of McCarthy's "secret": was he indeed an artist of politics, a genius who broods and bides his time while others babble, slowly acquiring in his own person a feel for the nation's deepest needs? And Kennedy: was he really brash and undeveloped, torn between passions of moral heroism and passions of personal power?

Better say right away the debate was inconclusive. Neither man had the imagination or the confidence totally to confront his opponent. Better say too that in the eyes of Eastern intellectuals, McCarthy had the better of it, because he was cool while Kennedy was undeniably cheap. Yet there was a way in which McCarthy lost that debate—lost as a man and as a leader.

The action opened with Kennedy accusing McCarthy "of forcing a coalition government on Saigon, a coalition with the Communists, even before we begin the negotiations." He himself would make it clear only that the Vietcong would "play some role" in the "future political process." In the meantime, he would start to replace American troops with South Vietnamese, demand an end to corruption and a beginning of land reform.

McCarthy said immediately, in his deeper, steadier voice: "I didn't say I was going to force a coalition government. . . . I said we should make it clear we are willing to accept that. Now, if the South Vietnamese want to continue to fight, work out their own negotiation, that is well and good, but I don't think there is much point in talking about reform in Saigon or land reform, because we have been asking for that for at least five years and it hasn't happened."

McCarthy had stood up strongly and scored on the first exchange. For a while Kennedy could not get himself settled —he was trying as usual to do too much. It was as though he'd been fed a tape that had gotten garbled: "If they haven't the will and the desire themselves, no matter what we do we can't instill in them, and that is why I want to make it clear if I was President of the United States—and why I was critical back in 1965 because I thought we were making it America's war, we were militarizing the conflict—that this is a South Vietnamese war. I am opposed to unilaterally withdrawing from there but they have to carry the major burden of the conflict."

Fifteen minutes into the hour it looked like Kennedy had panicked, while McCarthy was tough and ready.

Then they had a tight-lipped little fight about an ad which

ran in California implicating Kennedy not only in Vietnam, but in the Dominican intervention.* "I wasn't in the government at the time!" said Kennedy, correctly. McCarthy said he was talking about the "process" that led to Cuba and the Dominican Republic and Vietnam—although he had killed the ad as soon as he saw it. He shifted the subject to the Kennedy ads on the McCarthy voting record.

"I don't know to what he is referring," said Kennedy.

Then Kennedy began to pull himself together, working hard to say what he had come to say. He got in two mentions of obligations to Israel, said that the U.S. could not be the world's policeman, and mentioned the "astronomically high" property taxes "here in the state of California." When it came to the ghetto, he talked about "getting people jobs, just by giving the private sector tax incentives and tax credits." McCarthy meanwhile was abstract, aloof, as if he'd forgotten he were in a debate. Maybe his thought was that Kennedy had exposed himself and gotten rattled; now he could hold that contrast simply by keeping his dignity and lasting out the hour.

But Kennedy kept plugging. He wanted that private sector of his to rebuild both urban and rural areas: "so you keep people where they are at the present time."

McCarthy disagreed, following the theme of the Davis speech: "We have to get to the suburbs, too, with this kind of housing . . . because most of the employment is now in the belt line outside of the cities, and I don't think we ought

*This was an impassioned ad-man's embroidered version of the Cow Palace speech. It was, however, approved by Tom Finney. Perhaps political campaign ads should not be written by flacks. They usually are though.

to perpetuate the ghetto. . . . What we have got to do is to try to break that up. Otherwise, we are adopting a kind of apartheid in this country."

Kennedy had been waiting for this and he jumped in hard: "We have forty million [*sic*] Negroes who are in the ghettos at the present time. . . . You say you are going to take ten thousand black people and move them into Orange County. . . . If you are talking about hitting this problem in a major way, to take those people out, put them in the suburbs where they can't afford the housing, where their children can't keep up with schools, and where they don't have the skills for the jobs, it is just going to be catastrophic."

Appalled at Kennedy's excesses, we gleefully anticipated that McCarthy would come right back as he had on Vietnam, to say that he had never talked about ten thousand blacks in Orange County—which, incidentally, is a wealthy, lily-white residential area south of L.A., probably the most conservative county in the state. We were ready for him to hit at Kennedy for repeating some basic racial clichés, to point out that black children in integrated schools do not necessarily fall behind, that most of the new industrial jobs in the belt line require no skilled training, that he had called for public housing and new towns rather than simply throwing black people into areas they couldn't afford, and that merely gilding the ghetto cannot possibly provide jobs for all the unemployed there.

But McCarthy seemed baffled: ". . . I didn't want to raise —I thought that you really—when this position was first raised, that this was not your clear position of concentrating that much on the ghettos." Kennedy had hit him a hard shot on his basic policy for the cities, yet McCarthy did not defend himself.

A few minutes later, one of the questioners remarked on their lack of differences, and asked where they disagreed.

"I think we probably disagree some on Dean Rusk," said Senator McCarthy, "and on Robert McNamara and on some of the persons in government."

Kennedy hit again: "I think with all the problems that are affecting the United States, with the internal problems that we have and the problems around the rest of the world, to talk about it in terms of personality. . . . I don't want to be playing games with people's reputations."

McCarthy answered simply to say that he thought "we give Cabinet members too much protection." Once more Kennedy had caught him coasting and off-guard. "I think your brother was too kind to a number of people after the Bay of Pigs, myself," McCarthy said, but he did not make clear what he meant. He had slipped into a slur on John Kennedy without really defending his own position.

Kennedy was emboldened to press on, taking the role of an experienced and high-minded Cabinet officer who was bravely ignoring a slight to his brother and setting straight a reckless mudslinger. Kennedy was open for a sharp response —McCarthy might have gone into detail on the records of Rusk and McNamara. For months he had been talking wittily and effectively about leaders who personalized institutions; he might have made Kennedy defend that concept of office, forced him to cope with what was the most common public doubt about his candidacy. Instead McCarthy talked about how Rusk had alienated the Foreign Relations Committee.

Thus as the debate drew to an end, the roles had been completely reversed: Kennedy had had the guts to get up off the floor and fight it through, while McCarthy, dazed, was taking every punch. A minute later Kennedy gave some sharp figures on the way rich people evade taxes; McCarthy wobbled in technicalities: "I recommended early that they use other taxes, that they use credit controls and some selective excises instead of the surtax. . . ."

McCarthy was saved only by his sum-up. Thinking the debate was over, Kennedy was caught by surprise and inarticulate, while McCarthy reminded us that "in this year I sensed what this country needed . . . and I think there is something to be said for a President or a Presidential candidate who can somehow anticipate what the country wants, especially when what they want is on the side of good and justice. . . ."

On the basis of his sum-up, McCarthy's entourage went out happily crying up a victory for their very own candidate. Finney and his people knew the truth: the campaign had changed in Oregon, and now it had changed again. It was clear that Kennedy could take McCarthy head-on, with no fear of his magic powers. If McCarthy had something new and different going for him in American politics, it did not show in open competition with Kennedy. A few days later I learned of a private Kennedy survey: polling previously undecided voters in suburban areas where McCarthy had been getting stronger day by day, the survey found that the debate had swung these undecideds overwhelmingly to Kennedy.

35 THAT NIGHT THE PLUSH LOBBY OF THE FAIRMONT Hotel was jammed with McCarthy and Kennedy hangers-on, with newsmen, and with politicians, all of them seeking, seeking one another. All I could think was that I had three more days to go. After that, one of these men would win in behalf of the people and the values we had worked to represent. But neither of them deserved it.

I went off to dinner with a couple of famous people from the New Left—Bob Scheer and Tom Hayden. Scheer was decent to talk to—he wanted to interview McCarthy for *Ramparts*. *Ramparts* had even been a little bit impressed by McCarthy's attacks on the military. But Kennedy had been more gracious personally—inviting, conversing, and so on—and that counts, even with "revolutionaries." Hayden in his little fatigue cap was coming on as a personal representative of Uncle Ho. All of this McCarthy-Kennedy crap would be resolved by the emergence of the NLF in the United States. People like myself would be killed. Tough talk from a real revolutionary—or a beautiful put-on, just what "liberals" expect you to say: these were the two ways of admiring Tom Hayden.

"Why are you a whore for McCarthy?" was Hayden's greeting to me. Explain you are not a whore. I would have said I was acting in behalf of some good people in this country—but at that moment I was not nearly so sure of them as Hayden was of the American NLF.

I remember driving back to the hotel in someone's Volkswagen. Hayden was muttering, Scheer proposing, but my brain was dry from too many words and no music. After what I'd seen on that debate, I didn't much care for anyone's position. Despite myself, I swooned to catch the beat from the little Blaupunkt.

36 THE DAY AFTER THE DEBATE, WE WROTE UP A statement calling attention to the candidates' differences on Vietnam and accusing Kennedy of "scare tactics" on his "Orange County" business. Kennedy immediately replied, from Orange County, that "if Senator McCarthy thought I was not being precise, he had ample opportunity to respond when we were face-to-face."

On Vietnam, Kennedy began to say to his crowds, "Don't ask me why Gene McCarthy voted for the Tonkin Gulf resolution!" Tonkin Gulf came in the summer of '64, before Kennedy was in the Senate. He did not mention that McCarthy was one of five Senators who on March 1, 1966, voted to repeal that resolution—while Kennedy voted with the majority.

On election day, ads appeared quoting Kennedy "On Law Enforcement and Crime" and "On the Cities." Under McCarthy's name there appeared the notation, "Blank. Except for some good comments in the past few weeks."

That last day in California I was approached to join Kennedy as a speechwriter, in fact, to have breakfast with him the next morning. Mistakenly following the CBS estimate and anticipating a big win—nine percentage points—

which would all but eliminate McCarthy from contention, Kennedy was anxious to address himself to McCarthy's issue-oriented following. I replied that I felt I was wanted more as a defector than as a writer, that my main desire at the moment was to go home and leave these candidates to each other.

A few other young people near the top of the McCarthy organization were also invited to breakfast. Gorman declined, but Sam Brown, our "Youth Coordinator," accepted —from a sense of Kennedy's importance rather than from disloyalty—and Pierre Salinger got that impending meeting into the newspapers while voters were still going to the polls on June 4.

I did agree that the only two peace candidates should talk to one another, and agreed to suggest to McCarthy that he be receptive to a phone call from Kennedy—though I doubted that he would be. McCarthy, when he lost, made another we-shall-go-on statement, without mentioning Kennedy, just as in Indiana and Nebraska. Of course an open agreement with Kennedy at that point would have submerged his own candidacy.

Knowing the Democratic Party would be hard to convince, Kennedy had been interested from the beginning in some form of cooperation with McCarthy. Blair Clark, Curt Gans, and Richard Goodwin had foreseen that a bitter McCarthy-Kennedy contest might damage the unity of Democrats who opposed the war. They were receptive to some sort of understanding wherein Kennedy would campaign, say, in Indiana and Nebraska, McCarthy in Oregon—possibly each with the other's endorsement. The showdown would not come till California—an arrangement which might have given a different turn to the '68 campaign, a turn more favorable to peace.

After checking with McCarthy, Clark, Gans and Goodwin arranged to have Ted Kennedy fly at night and unattended to visit McCarthy in Green Bay during the Wisconsin campaign. McCarthy agreed to see Teddy. Then he tipped off David Schoumacher of CBS-TV, and went to bed. Teddy was greeted by an embarrassing moment on television, followed by the information that he was disturbing McCarthy's sleep. McCarthy received him—it made a funny story to tell later. In McCarthy's version, Teddy played the fool. The moral, at any rate, was no deal.

That night in Los Angeles, Bobby Kennedy wanted badly to join forces. He had an adviser phone Lowenstein in New York and Galbraith in Boston to ask whether he should travel across L.A. to see McCarthy. Then he went downstairs to make his best speech of the campaign, in which he talked modestly about how Americans had demonstrated their desire "for peace and for justice and for a government dedicated to giving the people mastery over their own affairs." He credited McCarthy and his supporters for "breaking the political logjam" and for making "citizen participation a new and powerful force in our political life." Commenting that Humphrey was leading in delegates without having debated the issues or submitted his candidacy to popular vote, he asked the McCarthy people to join with him "not for myself, but for the cause and the ideas which moved you to begin this great popular movement."

A few minutes later that great popular movement was ended for 1968, though we did not know it. The McCarthy kids had come to see their candidate at the Beverly Hilton. Now most of them were weeping; within a few minutes they were on the phones to their mothers back East. McCarthy himself paced up and down his suite while cops stood grimly at the door.

37 THERE WAS A MOMENT THEN, AT THE BEGINNING OF the summer, when Gene McCarthy was the only viable national leader. We had had a lame-duck President for two months: it was as if we did not have a President. Hubert Humphrey was tied up in fatuous professions of happiness and loyalty. Richard Nixon was a dark eminence, betting on the sober handshake, the thoughtful expression, and the strategy of saying nothing whatever. Nelson Rockefeller had played too cagey: he had lain low when it counted, and his last-minute barrage of PR grimmicks was not sufficient to communicate any deep sense of commitment.

Only Gene McCarthy had openly and steadily addressed himself to the central issue which so deeply disturbed America. Whether he believed in rapid structural change or not, his campaign had become a symbol for the "different direction" of which Robert Kennedy had spoken on that last night in the Ambassador Hotel. Now McCarthy was the only candidate of change. He was the only man who was in a position to tell America what had happened, to tell us who we were and what we must now do.

Dean Rusk seemed to speak for all the inadequacies of Humphrey and Nixon in his defensive statement on the assassination. "We must not," he said, "indict an entire people because of the wanton acts of certain violent individuals. The American people are a decent, wholesome, generous, and dedicated people who want to establish peace in the world and equality and social justice at home. But we have much unfinished business to which President Johnson has fully committed himself. . . . I know that John and Robert Kennedy would expect all of us to address ourselves to this unfinished business with all the wisdom and energy we can muster."

Unfinished business-as-usual, one might say. What had gone wrong with our decent, wholesome selves?

McCarthy began to tell us on the day after the assassination: "The nation, I think, bears too great a burden of guilt, really, for the kind of neglect which has allowed . . . violence to grow here in our land." He called this violence a "reflection of violence which we have visited upon the rest of the world, or at least on a part of the world." He said further that "We proceed as though we were still a pioneer country. We're not. We've become a rather complicated, sophisticated civilization"—implying that our neglect, our violence stemmed from a false and mythological self-image.

These few cryptic words seemed like the first efforts of a leader to fill the yearning for understanding and temperance which moved in our nation in the wake of three years of useless war and an assassin's bullet. Surely no politician had better credentials in restraint and dignity than Gene McCarthy held at that moment—or an evener tone with which to address the nation—or a clearer chance to press home the quiet advocacy of the values he believed in. If McCarthy had stepped forward at that moment with full presence and power, no one would have looked larger beside him.

But McCarthy could not, or would not, command his full power. The issues were not enough to maintain him, and the values which prevailed in him were not those which pertained to the state of America or the possibilities for leadership. He withdrew: and those few sentences on June 5 stood as tokens of the only time he glanced at the beast and told us what he saw.

38 McCARTHY DID NOT RESIGN HIS CANDIDACY; HE LEFT a lottery ticket in the big barrel to await the hand of God. But he never again addressed himself to the moment. He stood all summer passive and self-absorbed in the winding-down of his campaign. He had altered his style on the West Coast to suit the needs of scoring and winning. And what had it got him? Now in the heat of a lost, hot, vacant summer, while millions hoped for him and waited, Gene McCarthy regressed to his balanced presentation of self, to the sacred ceremony of his personality.

There was a political rationalization, which could be put on the spoons of a few favored journalists. McCarthy's only hope had been for a stalemate between Kennedy and Humphrey. With Kennedy gone, he simply could not match the machine connections. This ignored the fact that Humphrey was a loser, and that most of the party pros knew it—the very premise that Kennedy had been counting on. It ignored the availability of the Kennedy vote, which would hardly go to Humphrey as a matter of course. Finally, it did not acknowledge the possibility that the Democratic

Party would have to bend to public demand—the assumption on which the McCarthy movement was built, its proclaimed objective, and the power with which it had knocked out Johnson.

Finney, at least, thought there was a chance of politics. He came to McCarthy before they flew back from L.A. We've got to integrate our organization, he said. But he did not reckon on the price he had already exacted.—Well, said McCarthy, you boys see if you can integrate yourselves. You ought to call the President, Finney said. You call the President, said McCarthy.

Some of the younger people could rejoice in that last. McCarthy had shoved off the insiders, they thought, to go back to the people. They went home to join with folks who'd been knocking on the doors of state and local party caucuses for months. Fanned out across the nation, they waited for instructions from the man upstairs, to coordinate their efforts with his. If they were lucky, the man passed their way during the summer; they could go and look at him and hold up two fingers and cheer. But the instructions never came.

39 IT WAS JUNE 12 BEFORE MCCARTHY SPOKE AGAIN. I went down to Washington with my head throbbing to a phrase which had been thrusting from radios all spring: "Where have you gone, Joe DiMaggio, a nation turns its hungry eyes to you." My retirement plans had been premature. One could not let go of McCarthy now; he was—

as we were to hear over and over and ever more sadly as the summer slipped by—our only hope.

On June 11 the mood was tight but the possibilities were still very real. McCarthy was to reopen his campaign in the Senate Building the next day. Was it possible Gorman and I could get to him with a statement? His Senate office insisted he was not to be reached, but we left word we would bring him something later.

Unsure of our commission, we worked with difficulty, hoping at best to touch all the bases. Our first assumption was that he would speak in the Senate caucus room—where he could invoke the memory of his first announcement and of Robert Kennedy's.

He could begin by recounting what had happened since then: Johnson dropping, the opening of negotiations, the two assassinations, further violence in our cities. The theme was that the crisis had intensified: anxiety deepening, people losing faith and hope. It was a time for still greater commitment to our original principles. "We call for change in America because without change we fear for our nation's future."

The talks in Paris were getting nowhere—and our position remained inflexible. The fighting continued, so did the dying. McCarthy would go on talking about Vietnam. Not merely because policies required changing, but because it was time to think about the lessons of Vietnam—to understand what it tells us about ourselves as a people, about our leaders and institutions.

Likewise he would talk about the crisis of our cities, the problems of black people and poor people. The loss of

Kennedy and King made that discussion all the more essential.

Behind these lay deeper questions, involving our capacity for peaceful change or for shattering violence. For discontent was growing in America. Voices which cried for justice and liberation had been ignored. Citizens were excluded from the processes of government. "Discontent in America grows as much from a sense of powerlessness as from poverty. It is a discontent with the present state of our democracy."

It was this condition to which McCarthy had originally addressed his candidacy—and the American people had shown in the primaries that they were ready to renew democracy and to revitalize its processes. They had made their will known—the question now was whether our political parties could respond to that will.

McCarthy had faith that they would—at least he did in our statement. He had confidence in America. He believed that democracy would prevail—"in the Democratic Party and in the country which it serves."

It was after dark when we drove out to McCarthy's house. He was not at home—maybe he would be cut off now for good from his campaign. But we found him around the block at the home of Gil Harrison, publisher and editor of *The New Republic*, sitting in the den with Harrison and Harrison's teen-age son. A Secret Service man stood outside the door; two more waited at the curb.

McCarthy was shocking: deep hollows cut under his eyes, his face was ravaged and grim—as if he hadn't slept for a week. He told us about how he had been to see Johnson that day. They had sat just the two of them at a huge conference table. "He told me the Vietcong are getting desperate—making a last-ditch stand. We're going to negotiate from strength. The same old stuff." He shrugged his head, dug his hands into his eyes.

But he seemed glad we had found him, relieved to have that statement. He read it carefully. "I think this is about right," he said.

But immediately he cut out all the references to Kennedy. Harrison, the staunchest of McCarthy men, pressed him to say something positive about Kennedy, to appeal directly and honestly to Kennedy's followers, who were waiting to see how McCarthy would react, and to Kennedy's delegates, who were already being approached by Humphrey. Or else the game might be over right away.

"I thought I just wouldn't mention Bobby," McCarthy said. "Well, I won't make him my lead."

Possibly he thought it was bad taste to be appealing to people in the name of his rival of just a week ago—the motive would seem personal. Finally I suggested he keep just the reference to Kennedy and King (two of our greatest men, lost voices who had spoken to us of poverty and the crises of our cities), and he did. Then he asked me to put in a sentence about how the Administration had ignored the Foreign Relations Committee.

To my amazement, Harrison began asking McCarthy if he felt guilty about the assassination. "No," McCarthy said, "everything I said about him was completely fair."

He was reluctant to talk about it, dropping into depression again, but Harrison kept on, working against McCarthy's grain in a way we knew was dangerous.

"If I were you, Gene, I'd feel just a little guilty—it's irrational, but all the same—how could you help it?"

Of course he feels guilty, I thought. What else would do that to him? Maybe Harrison wanted to help him face it.

But McCarthy shook his heavy head. "He said he didn't enter New Hampshire because his personality would get in the way, then he came to Oregon with his dog and his astronaut. So it was perfectly fair."

He stared dully at the pages on his lap. Across the room Harrison's son was scoring LBJ, who had said that the violence must stop, but hadn't said how.

McCarthy lifted his head. "Who's that?" he said. "Bobby?"

Harrison tried a joke about how certain columnists were always speculating that something was wrong with McCarthy.

McCarthy seemed not to hear him.

"There's something wrong with McCarthy all right," he murmured to himself. "But they don't know what it is."

40 McCARTHY HAD TAKEN OUR COPY TO LOOK IT OVER once more. In the morning he would have it run off and distributed.

It is a beautiful summer day that next morning. We come to the Hill in some anticipation. McCarthy has been disturbed about the campaign up to now—but today he can make a new beginning.

We learn later that the statement was mimeoed and a few reporters were walking off with it when the secretary came after them and snatched it out of their hands. But all we know at the time is that no one has it. "What text?" people shrug, and someone tells us McCarthy has thrown it out. He has canceled the caucus room as well.

We race down to the Agriculture Committee hearing room, one of the smallest in the building—and come upon a hundred reporters milling out in the hall, unable to get in. The fifty-foot room is jammed with press people, the ones in back crushing up because they can't hear or see, the ones in front leaning with mikes and cameras. I can just see McCarthy's head, which is down. He is sitting at a table. No, he waves off the microphone. He begins to mumble into the tabletop.

He says he will continue "a limited campaign." He doesn't feel that the assassination has changed anything. He mentions Kennedy to say that, "The response to my candidacy, and also to that of Senator Kennedy, rather clearly demonstrated, I think, the popular response."

When the floor is open, he flattens each question as fast as it comes.

Would he "welcome a series of discussions or confrontations or debates on the issues" with the Vice President?

"If at some point," McCarthy says, "he feels that the positions I am taking ought to be challenged, why, we will then have to decide how best to present the differences, or to receive his challenge, to the public for their judgment."

Does he think Humphrey will lose ground if he doesn't speak on the issues?

"I don't really know. . . ."

Now and later, he will not challenge Humphrey.

"What argument can you make to these undecided

delegates? Why should they vote for you rather than Humphrey?"

"I don't think I will make that argument to them. I will simply ask them to be responsible delegates and to make the judgment that has to be made in August, which is a question of what issues the Democratic Party is going to support at that time; and then to ask the question as to which candidate is likely best to carry those issues to the country. I just ask them for a reserved judgment."

Does he perhaps have any plans to appeal to the Negro vote?

"I never looked upon that as an area in which I should really very seriously contest with Senator Kennedy, although people tried to raise that issue. We did try to get to them what my record was. And it is a good record; I have no problems about that. . . . And I have never had any problem about minority support in my own state."

I walk to McCarthy's office with a sympathetic fund-raiser who is explaining to me that now is not the best time to mention things that bother people. McCarthy knows what he is doing.

"And besides," I say, "he is our only hope."

"That's right. And don't you forget it!"

Back in the office the secretary is pleased to inform us that McCarthy has left already. Knowing that he is scheduled to make his first speech the next day at the Community Council of Greater New York, he asked her to get out his blue-plate special from 1961, a history of poverty among the Greeks and Romans, with a description of welfare as practiced among medieval monasteries. An elderly office aide is engaged in writing up a press release on "the four new civil rights," which he is copying from a statement dated 1959. McCarthy has left behind some papers, which the secretary takes from his desk for me to bring to him.

On McCarthy's desk is a book by Camus, open to an essay on "The Responsibility of the Artist." In times of stress, Camus writes, the artist must be careful not to debase his language—because it is all he's got. That passage is marked. But it makes no mention of politicians.

41 IN THE NEXT WEEK MCCARTHY MADE A SERIES OF cryptic proclamations which pushed him further into isolation. First he said he was going to Paris sometime during the summer. When reporters asked him if he would talk to American negotiators or whether he had contacts with the North Vietnamese, his answers were unclear.

Then on June 14, he found it necessary to say that Americans were ready to welcome "unilateral withdrawal"—and had to explain that he was not advocating it, just trying to say how unpopular the war had become. It was the kind of point that could be appreciated only by those who already agreed with him.

On June 16, when asked about the drive for gun control which had followed the assassination, McCarthy said, "It's been my experience in twenty years in the Congress that you really ought not to put through legislation under panic conditions." The *Washington Post* wondered what McCarthy had done about gun control during twenty years of non-panic. If he thought it over long and hard, he could not have chosen anything better calculated to alienate Kennedy people. The statement was more than just a political mistake, more than a random expression of McCarthy's procedural conservatism. Twist and turn it as you would, there was a kind of meanness beyond excuse or explanation.

There was a particular pressure during those early days of the summer for McCarthy to make a personal appeal to Negro voters who felt lost without Kennedy. In the weeks that followed, Norval Reece scheduled frequent appearances in big city ghettos. But by this time McCarthy had been taken over by the Secret Service (whose code word for him was "snowstorm"). Usually when a ghetto appearance was scheduled, the Secret Service would point to a violent encounter between militants and police such as occurred in every ghetto every weekend all summer long. They would phone McCarthy's secretary in the Senate office, and she would cancel the appearance. In Pittsburgh, McCarthy overruled the Secret Service, but in Newark, Detroit, Los Angeles, and other places, he did not go.

42 ON JUNE 18 THE NEW YORK PRIMARY GAVE MCCARTHY what he himself said later was the most meaningful victory of the campaign, a practical demonstration of the power of the new politics. For instead of voting for candidates, the voters had to select three delegates in each of 41 districts—which meant that the McCarthy movement in New York State (the Committee for a Democratic Alternative, led by Harold Ickes and Sarah Kovner) had to run 41 campaigns,

identifying 123 delegates with McCarthy and explaining door-to-door what that meant in terms of the issues.

The CDA pulled a kind of grass-roots support that the Democratic machine simply could not match. Sixty-two McCarthy delegates were elected, 30 Kennedy delegates, 19 uncommitted, and only 12 delegates for Humphrey. In addition, Paul O'Dwyer, an antiwar McCarthy supporter, upset strong Kennedy and Humphrey men in the senatorial primary, suggesting that McCarthy had coattails.

Yet all that week the man himself had said that the primaries were over. He would not even accept a phone call from Ickes and Kovner. Now the CDA in New York was used to going it alone: they had built an independent organization, defended it from the encroachments of national organizers, and faithfully raised money to send up to New Hampshire or down to Washington. Ickes and Kovner had already given up on meeting with their candidate or receiving direction from him on their relations with the New York Democratic Party. By now they asked only one thing: that the candidate simply come to a New York rally to identify himself with his delegates and to ask people to vote for them.

But McCarthy would not do it.

In despair the New York people turned to Erich Fromm, who had lectured in behalf of McCarthy, organized social scientists to support him, and written a speech which McCarthy delivered on June 12 at the Fellowship of Reconciliation. On the night of June 16, Fromm began to telephone McCarthy. He was told by the secretary and again by the valet that McCarthy could not be disturbed. Then he was informed by a psychiatrist friend in McCarthy's entourage that he had no business meddling in politics.

Finally McCarthy was prevailed upon to take Fromm's call. He did not say no in person. He came to New York for an election eve rally in Lewisohn Stadium. He didn't say much about the primary, or the Poor People's March in Washington that next week, but he did say it was time to take our steel from the land of thatched huts, our tanks from the land of the water buffalo, our napalm from a land which barely knew the use of matches.

The primary victory the next night might have given us a strong push toward renewing the campaign. It made a tremendous impression on press and politicians. But not on McCarthy, who remained in a funk.

43 WE SPENT MUCH OF THE SUMMER FLYING TO STATE conventions—where McCarthy would repeat pretty much what he'd said all along—and ask political leaders, much to their astonishment and not without condescension, to keep an open mind. McCarthy would not critize Humphrey, except to say he didn't have a position on Vietnam. He knew if he weakened Humphrey, and Humphrey got the nomination, he could be accused of making Nixon President. But Humphrey was now his direct and only opponent. The reasons for fighting Humphrey were just as good as the reasons for going into New Hampshire.

Usually Humphrey came to speak to the same convention,

but there was never a debate; the two men would speak at different times and decorously ignore one another. Young people would pack the galleries for McCarthy, and middle-aged party regulars for HHH. Humphrey was the Dagwood Bumstead of politicians: anything good he heard from anyone else, he would cram into his sandwich of a speech, spread it with a layer of schmaltz, and gulp the whole thing down. He talked, for instance, about a "participation politics" while party regulars were closing caucuses, stealing delegations, and ignoring primaries in Connecticut, Pennsylvania, Massachusetts, Indiana, Missouri, Texas, Minnesota, etc. When McCarthy was prevailed upon to criticize the handling of hunger in America, the lack of U.S. pressure to stop the genocide in Biafra, or the jailing of Dzu in South Vietnam, the next day Humphrey would say the same thing, and twice as sincerely, just as if he were not part of the government whose inaction he deplored.

"I'm dying to go after Humphrey," McCarthy said in July. "When I read those speeches I think if only he were a Republican . . ."

"Why not go after him as if he were?" I asked.

"I will."

But he couldn't. All summer we carried around a specially-prepared "book" on Humphrey: McCarthy never used it. Unlike Kennedy, who had vowed to "chase Hubert's ass around the country," McCarthy must have recognized some kinship with Humphrey. He joked about how he himself had come close to being in Humphrey's shoes (though he said he would have kept silent, or retired). Despite his contempt for Hubert's hawkery and his tears, he seemed to know that all the same, the man was trapped.

Then, too, in terms of the "politics of effectiveness," Humphrey was a success. Being McCarthy's senior senator, he had pre-empted the field as the Senate's most active liberal. "Every time McCarthy started to climb the ladder," says a Washington insider, "he found Humphrey's ass staring him in the face." All the more reason to give that ass a boot, unless, as Tom Finney still believes, McCarthy had a lingering respect for Humphrey's legislative ability. "If he thought," says Finney, "that one of the other candidates might just be a better President than himself, that man was Hubert Humphrey." Months after the campaign was over, I learned that in the beginning, McCarthy had told a Washington acquaintance that he would be happy if 1968 ended with Humphrey running for President on a peace plank. My first thought was that the Coos Bay slip on Humphrey had been no slip, and that our Cow Palace speech had indeed served the ends of deception.

The final irony of McCarthy's forebearance toward Humphrey is that—as McCarthy himself anticipated—Humphrey backers, especially the labor people, bitterly blamed McCarthy for losing Humphrey the election. McCarthy gave a late endorsement carefully limited to Humphrey's better understanding of racial problems and the dangers of the arms race. But the mystery to those in the McCarthy movement is how Humphrey could expect anything more from McCarthy and his followers when he renounced neither the war nor the brutality in Chicago. A stronger endorsement would have changed no minds, but it would have instantly destroyed whatever remained of McCarthy's credibility with whatever remained of his movement. It was inevitable, given Humphrey and the position he had to uphold, that a certain number of liberals were simply not going to recognize him as a lesser evil than Richard Nixon. They would argue that Nixon, at least, had no stake in justifying Johnson's policies (though he had wanted us to go into Indochina in 1954). And should the Democratic Party be rewarded with victory after having ignored and even suppressed the preference of Democratic voters? (How the Democratic Party would reward their abstention was another matter.) Probably most antiwar liberals—though not enough —did in the end vote against Nixon, but during the summer their candidate showed a kind of good faith toward the man they were hoping to beat that would have dismayed them if they had seen it.

44 BY THE MIDDLE OF THE SUMMER, MCCARTHY HAD severed his contact with his movement: they were reduced to faces at airports and rallies, and the man made cracks to reporters about the "ski-bums" who had joined his campaign. Supposedly he was now going to concentrate on the delegates and politicians, to approach them and bargain for power. In reality, however, the candidate could not do this and would not authorize anyone to do it for him.

Really it was the McCarthy movement that should have done the bargaining. After all, it represented McCarthy's popular base (if not his full drawing power as a candidate). Some of it was already within the party, with more on its way, and it had developed a campaign structure that in many states was more effective than the Democratic "machine." In fact, the movement was a political force which any Democratic candidate would need to win. It could offer the Democrats organization, numbers, and a future. If the Democrats could have worked out some means of accommodation, they would have saved their party some legitimate claim to relevance. They would have shown that the Democratic Party could respond to the authentic problems and needs which America in 1968 was trying simultaneously to confront and to avoid. If McCarthy could have shown this to his party, he could have served as the fulcrum of a bargain —to his advantage and to everyone's.

There were legitimate reasons, too, for going to the Governors and other politicians of the Democratic Party. (a) The original objective of the McCarthy campaign was to bring pressure for change within the party. Therefore at some point someone had to demand recognition and power in that arena. In practice, this was left to brave and isolated state caucuses. (b) Assuming that McCarthy would have made a stronger candidate than Humphrey—and politicians were not so dull that they could not imagine it —the question remained as to what role various Democratic officeholders and party men would play in the campaign and in a new Administration, all the way down to the local level. Certainly it was legitimate for professionals who had devoted their lives to politics to want to know, in the words of Dick Goodwin, "whether they would be playing shortstop or sitting on the bench." (c) Finally, they did legitimately represent some people, even where they had not been chosen democratically. There is no doubt that the party regulars in many localities had close contact with the communities they came from and more accurately represented the interests of the different groups that composed them than did the McCarthy insurgents.

For a moment that summer, McCarthy was in a unique position to bring together the two halves of what might be the Democratic Party. In failing to do so, he deprived his "constituency of conscience" the opportunity to follow up on what they had begun in New Hampshire and Wisconsin—to make common cause with the bread-and-butter America of small farms, trade unions, and ethnic groups. There can be no doubt that bringing these two halves together was the political objective of Robert Kennedy. Perhaps without him, it could not have been done. Perhaps the war and the defensiveness of the Administration would have driven an impassable wedge. Or perhaps the benefits of turning from the war would have been irresistible. But we never found out, because McCarthy confined the issues to his own personality. "I am the cause now," he said privately. He wasn't going about like a crusader, he was merely offering himself in case the infidels cared for conversion. Since that was unlikely, who could blame him for staying above the party, above his own movement, and beyond the possibility of power?

45 AFTER THE ASSASSINATION TWO STRATEGIES WERE PROposed to McCarthy. Tom Finney wanted to hunt delegates in the standard manner, stressing McCarthy's vote-getting abilities and his record as a party man who could cooperate with party regulars. He wanted to assure the delegates that

McCarthy's rebellion was based on opposition to the war and a desire to open the party to greater participation—but *not* on any notion of "junking the party." He knew that Lyndon Johnson was not crazy about Humphrey, and hoped that he might privately agree to remain neutral—in which case the delegates branded for Humphrey (and Finney counted 1800 of them), might cut loose overnight. The result would be that without unnecessarily offending Johnson, McCarthy might quietly rescue the Democratic Party and lead it to a more realistic and attractive position on Vietnam.

Stephen Mitchell—who had been party chairman during the Stevenson years—wanted to put pressure on the party through popular challenges, public exposure, and demonstrations of grass-roots strength. "Our only chance," says Mitchell, "was to fight every damn thing we could, and bring the public to the point where they would bear on the delegates." Mitchell came to Chicago with a maximum number of challenges under way on the premise that "you have to start subsidiary fights in a convention if you are to capture that convention." The majority that was brought around on abolishing the "Unit Rule" suggested to him a potential majority for McCarthy. He wanted to oppose the Administration on the first day by nominating Jesse Unruh of California as convention chairman in opposition to Carl Albert. Kennedy and McGovern delegates would have joined in on the effort, and Humphrey, forced to stick to Albert, would have lost what support he had in California. The unity and purpose of the McCarthy movement would have dominated the proceedings. With the American public tuned in to the drama on TV, there would be intense pressure on the delegates. Finally McCarthy himself would take the convention floor.

Finney and Mitchell had something in common: their absolute loyalty to the Democratic Party. Both knew that the party structure had been weakened in different ways by John Kennedy and Lyndon Johnson, who tended to operate on the strength of their own personalities. Both wanted McCarthy—as one who was concerned with procedures and balances—to present a positive vision of rebuilding the party.

The difference was that getting political leverage through public pressure was utterly foreign to Finney. His strategy called for discretion rather than criticism, and the tacit elimination of the movement and its managers. Mitchell, however, felt that McCarthy had to coordinate his efforts with the network of young staff people and grass-roots organizations operating roughly and sometimes rebelliously under the direction of Curt Gans. Finney argued that you could not pressure or challenge delegates you were wooing to vote for you. Mitchell argued that we couldn't compete on that basis with Humphrey's connections. Perhaps the points of view were not irreconcilable, if there were the kind of leadership which would carefully decide where to bargain and where to pressure.

Various meetings and conferences were held now and then throughout the summer supposedly to decide just that question. The candidate listened and nodded and usually approved. Amazingly, all parties left their meetings confident that the nod of the McCarthy head had gone to them. Evans and Novak were leaked a story that Finney had taken charge, after "McCarthy was dragged—kicking and screaming—into conventional politics." Finney, however, never did get started. He held out for sole control of the delegate operation, and McCarthy would not give it to him—or to anyone else.

Steve Mitchell asked McCarthy four times from May to July if he would support his efforts to open the convention and finally take the floor in person. Every time McCarthy was enthusiastic. I myself remember an hour's ride on the freeways with McCarthy on the last day of California. "We'll have fun, won't we, Jeremy?" he said as he described how he would challenge the convention. He asked me what I thought of his announcing immediately that he was releasing all his delegates, as the first step to fight the Unit Rule. I told him he better wait till Chicago. I would not have believed how little he would care by then.

Curtis Gans, for his part, felt or wanted to feel that the Mitchell strategy had been adopted, and on the strength of that asked McCarthy's permission to bring together a convention of grass-roots supporters. Backed by Blair Clark, he spent thousands of dollars bringing local leaders and staff from all over the country to Chicago in the middle of June. The meeting was chaotic—many people wanted to know just what was the relationship between Gans, Mitchell and Finney. Who had the authority to do what, and on whose mandate were they called together? Where was McCarthy and what was his commitment? They were not enthusiastic about Gans' idea for a national petition, and that project never materialized. Gans had understood that McCarthy would come and speak to those who had worked hardest for him. But McCarthy stayed in Washington and ridiculed Gans and his convention—though he could have stopped it with a word.

And he could have substituted . . . anything he liked.

46 IN CALIFORNIA, McCARTHY'S ENTOURAGE HAD BEEN joined by a former advance man who wore his hair in a Pinocchio bowl-cut and who acted as a court jester. Pinocchio played a leading role on the campaign plane, which by the middle of the summer was an appalling experience for the serious young campaign workers who hitched a lift from one city to another. McCarthy could have surrounded himself with the cream of American intellectuals, almost all of whom supported him—or with an array of experts on America's political problems—or with the most talented and attractive of the younger generation of politicians—but instead he let his plane fill up with snobs, sycophants, stooges, and clowns. Much of the time there was not a single adviser of any political experience on the plane. It got so bad that from June only a handful of reporters stuck with us. Despite everything that McCarthy had accomplished in 1968, when newsmen traveled with him they simply could not believe he was seriously running for President.

It was an American Airlines charter, with beer and shrimp, lobster and champagne, hors d'oeuvres and California grapes. The atmosphere was that of a Sunday school picnic for snotty rich kids. The Harvard boy and his chum joked about the campaign with their favorite reporters as if it were a marvelous put-on. There were no press releases, no sense that the candidate would respond to current developments. McCarthy sat up front with the psychiatrist friend and one or two others who were clearly not friends in any sense of equality—and allowed his loyal retainers to mediate between himself and the outer world. Now and then a reporter would venture forward to pick up some nasty cracks about other politicians. McCarthy had a one-liner for everyone in Washington, and the reporters who found favor were those who learned to leer and feed straight lines.

Through all of this, Pinocchio would wander, dressed in pilot's goggles and remnants of rubber water clothes. Sometimes he made witty announcements on the P-A about the excretory habits of someone on board. He thought it was a gas to walk up the aisle slapping people with a towel. When he got McCarthy's bags to the hotel he would make a specialty of snapping out orders to the local volunteers who came to help and worship.

Contacts were suggested with people of political or intellectual reputation, but invariably these people had been soft on Bobby at one time or another and were tainted with "opportunism." Once Gorman came up with an idea for a "poverty tour." He proposed that McCarthy announce an itinerary of city ghettos, Indian reservations, Mexican farm camps, plantations, Appalachian mining districts, sharecrop rural areas. He would invite local and national leaders who spoke for the poor to travel with him for one stop or for all week. He would take a temporary staff of experts who had written most convincingly on aspects of poverty. Then after the trip he would make a major address, perhaps on national TV, summarizing his impressions and setting forth concrete proposals.

I suppose the trouble was that such a tour could be construed as a belated effort to follow in Bobby's footsteps. McCarthy replied without interest that he was "willing" to go to "these places," but only in the way he went to other places. The "traveling circus" continued.

In Oklahoma, McCarthy staff and local people had arranged for him to get at least six delegates. But McCarthy came to the convention in Oklahoma City and told the party leaders that he only needed two or three, just so he was represented. Mitchell phoned to get him to come to Little Rock, saying there was a chance for 30 to 40 delegates—but McCarthy couldn't make it.

One day the plane sat in the airport at Des Moines, waiting for McCarthy to return from addressing the state convention and asking delegates brought to his suite to keep an open mind. Some of McCarthy's attendants were playing baseball on the grass between the runways. When McCarthy arrived they immediately relinquished the bat to him and retreated some 400 feet. There was no question of his actually playing—without removing his coat he carefully took his position while two aides competed to throw him a soft one. But soon there was trouble—McCarthy refused to swing at the pitches because they were not in the strike zone. Every once in a while he would swing but he did not connect solidly, and thereafter would wait even longer before swinging again. Meanwhile one suitor would wrench the ball from the next in anxiety to be the one who could groove it for Daddy.

At last McCarthy hit a long pop and strode into the plane. He saw me watching. "Regulation distance!" he said. And when his retinue caught up: "Next time the mound has to be regulation distance!"

47 FROM DES MOINES WE FLEW TO LANSING AND THE Michigan state convention. The next night McCarthy had an important speech scheduled in Chicago, and Gorman had phoned me from Washington with a text on the political process, scoring Humphrey's undemocratic delegate raids and challenging the party to respond to the primaries. It might have been important: I spent my time in Lansing editing the text and going over it with McCarthy. Meanwhile one of the best McCarthy advance men, Tony Podesta, a grad student from MIT, had gone into Lansing a few days ahead of us, arranged for a tremendous crowd to fill two hangars at the airport, and learned all about the power structure in the state of Michigan. The next morning. Sunday, June 30, Podesta had arranged for McCarthy to meet a selected group of liberal labor leaders and other delegates who were interested and, for the most part, uncommitted.

Podesta rode to the meeting in the car with McCarthy and the valet, supposedly to brief the candidate on the people he would encounter. "I knew," said Podesta, "that he switches off right away. I'd decided that you can only tell him one thing. So all the way in the car I kept telling him that what these guys cared about most was whether he was a good Democrat. They had their doubts about the war and so on—but they wanted to know if he would lead the party."

Of course McCarthy had put in twenty years of being a loyal Democrat. But maybe he didn't like being briefed by a twenty-four-year-old, maybe he didn't believe the delegates were really open. Maybe it was just that he was a sucker for a hypothetical question—in this case an inquiry from Gus Scholle, head of the State AFL-CIO, as to whether he might conceivably support Rockefeller. This is a question that would naturally occur in advance to any politician in McCarthy's position, and if you are seeking the Democratic nomination your answer is absolutely not. But to Podesta's horror, McCarthy took the question as an academic exercise, and started to comment on the circumstances in which he might find Rockefeller's programs "acceptable." From that moment he was through, as far as his listeners were concerned, and Podesta could see it in their faces.

And that night's speech was through, too, even though McCarthy threw in his first really positive remark on Kennedy. For the *Chicago Sun-Times* headlined McCARTHY DROPS A HINT HE COULD SUPPORT ROCKY*—and the criticism of Humphrey, the challenge to the party, were washed out in Monday morning papers all over the country.

At the Lansing meeting was Zoltan Ferency, state chairman of the Democratic Party through December, 1967, the only state chairman to come out for McCarthy and an early opponent of the war, who held the first meeting of the Conference of Concerned Democrats in Michigan in the spring of 1967. Ferency knew that Scholle was an old

*McCarthy has told friends that after the Democratic Convention Rockefeller telephoned his Senate office four times, but he did not return the call.

Humphrey man who had tried deliberately to strike out McCarthy. Said Ferency, without surprise, "Scholle threw him a curve and he missed it."

McCarthy as usual said he was misquoted. He was mad at Podesta, too. "I heard I was on his shit list," Tony said. "Pinocchio told me."

48 WHEREVER WE WENT THERE WOULD BE A GROUP OF black leaders who wanted to talk to McCarthy privately—to get the feel of him and to see how he would acknowledge them. It was tough on McCarthy. Despite his insistence that black people get to know his record, his appeal, as we have seen, was very much involved with the formal presentation of his personality. In a small group the formality could be chillingly impersonal, and with non-white or non-college people the presentation simply didn't take.

In a certain way McCarthy and the black leaders had a lot in common. Both he and they had placed tremendous importance on style as the chief sign of substance. Words and trappings were important on both sides, but different words, different trappings. Like many a black man, McCarthy began an encounter with the feeling of having been slighted, and waited for the other to make gestures of appreciation. When gestures were not forthcoming, the original impression was confirmed on either side.

Yet on the part of the black leaders there was a touching desire to make contact, hopefully, to deal. The death of Kennedy had severed their main line of hope. And despite all the talk of separation and the threats of violence, the black community had to seek out contact. For it truly was, as McCarthy said, dependent on white support even to finance its separatism.* The greatest disaster for them in terms of a Presidential election would be the success of a candidate who owed them nothing whatsoever. They had to talk.

In more ways than one, however, the conversation was not what it was assumed to be. Theoretically, the black leaders would deliver the support of their communities if they found McCarthy acceptable. Actually there was a question not only about delivery but even about whom a given leader represented. Some of the people were leaders mainly by virtue of their attendance at meetings like these—and how was McCarthy to tell the difference?

Often the McCarthy advance staff would contact the black leadership in each new city, and I would get an urgent phone call describing what phrases had to be included in the next night's speech if the black leadership was to endorse McCarthy. Usually it was a matter of emotion, not words, and McCarthy never got through to black people with enough force to make it profitable for the leadership to endorse him. Then, too, he not only refused to make deals, he was a poor prospect for power. It did no harm, though, to contact him, or to play with whoever approached in his behalf. For self-protection one had to be ready to make one's move with any candidate in reach.

Before McCarthy was to come to Detroit on July 27, I was bombarded by phone calls from Podesta and his helpers, who put live black leaders on the line with me. Some of

*In this way the separatist language is used as a hedge to allow black people to take white money and use white support without feeling debased or entering into competition.

them spoke for Reverend Cleage, a real power, but others I wasn't sure of. They told me the key words were "transfer of power"—if McCarthy would say these words, they would guarantee to fill Tiger Stadium with black people. But even I was amused at the notion that we could swing the whole community on the strength of an advance text.

I was working on a speech about how the Democratic Party could once again become "the party of the people," putting in as many specific programs as possible, to impress the professionals that McCarthy did have programs and did see himself as a leader of the party. It was easy enough to add that the Democratic Party must "bring about a transfer of power, so that black people can run their own communities and form an effective base from which to participate in the politics of the larger community. Since we have isolated black people, we must give them the opportunity to govern themselves, etc." But when McCarthy read this he said, "Yes, but how? You just can't do it." And properly he crossed it out.

What government could do is to set up local participation in running health and child-care facilities, schools and job-training centers—and McCarthy left those paragraphs in. I knew from experience he would never say them—possibly because he thought it was wrong to suggest that these techniques would in any real way solve the basic problems of the ghetto. Then again, he was not interested in the possibilities of that sort of participation—he never tried himself to say how a new politics might apply to life in the ghetto.

Nevertheless the rhetoric about "powerlessness" and the practical suggestions for participation which McCarthy let stand were strong enough to impress my phone contacts—and supposedly the Detroit ghetto was ours.

But what do you know, 98 percent of the audience in Tiger Stadium the next night was "upper-middle-class whites," according to the *Michigan Daily*. Anyhow, the text was circulated to black leaders, who said they were impressed. And on his final trip to Los Angeles, McCarthy was introduced to a well-dressed white dinner crowd at the Beverly Hilton by a black man who said, "They say this man has nothing to say about black people!"—and then glowingly read the words McCarthy never said about black people being "poor because they are powerless and powerless because they are black," and so on into the ideas McCarthy never had on how to change life in the ghetto.

Once in New York, McCarthy completely stupefied a group of Negro publishers with reminiscences of the 1948 campaign and his political hero, Harry Truman. Once again, his thesis was that we cannot begin to deal with our racial problems until we fulfill the basic commitments we undertook in 1948 and reaffirmed in the Kerner Report.

He was right, but they weren't listening. All the rightness in the world means little unless a politician can take his views to the people, can relate them to the way they experience the problem, and can persuade them that his solution fits their needs. McCarthy's problem on the Negro question was that he simply could not convince anyone he cared. "Caring" for him was a matter of accepting obligation. For McCarthy's secular movement, and especially for black people, "caring" was a matter of contact, a matter of firsthand involvement. I personally believe that McCarthy as President would have known the right thing and tried to do it. I'm less sure about the consistency of his efforts, but at any rate he would have been better for black America than a politician who cheers black capitalism and drools to hug black babies, and who then comes up short with the bread and butter. Still, in the narrowest sense in which he was accused, McCarthy could not make contact, he did not personally identify.

Critics used to complain that he "lacked compassion." McCarthy, scornful of feelings worn on the sleeve, referred to this as "the compassion gap."

I remember a typical occurrence in Atlanta, where the crowd along the airport fence was composed of cheering black schoolchildren. After shaking hands briefly, McCarthy walked along the fence at a distance of several yards, nodding his head and waving one hand from his hip and his lapel, keeping two Secret Service men between him and them, then veering away before he got fifty yards from the end. We drove to a rundown Atlanta slum called Vine City, where several cooperatives have tried to take up the slack of poverty. But McCarthy wasn't interested in looking around, for the street was filled with grinning black children.

With his valet clearing a path, McCarthy moved straight from his limousine to the small frame house which served as a community center, where he was supposed to give a little talk. In one minute he came out and plowed straight back to his car. Otherwise the children would gladly have entertained him for an hour in the street. Perhaps McCarthy felt he didn't deserve them; he knew his advance men could have pulled them for any candidate. Perhaps to stop would have made him a demagogue. But it's a pity he had nothing to ask, nothing to learn, nothing to enjoy.

49 That brief southern tour in the middle of July turned out to be McCarthy's most hopeful moment of the summer. For one last week he again believed he might be President. Humphrey was looking more and more like a loser. A few days before we started, the Harris poll took a sampling of 1500 voters on personal traits of McCarthy and Humphrey, and McCarthy scored higher in every category. Seventy–two percent thought he was sincere, as compared to 59 percent for Humphrey; in straightforwardness it was 67 to 54 percent; cool-headedness, 70–52; decisiveness, 59–42; being worthy of confidence, 52–43; independence 75–42; "up-to-date ideas," 53–42; capacity to be exciting, 34–27; and good looks, 63–21. Said Harris: "Two facts emerge sharp and clear. . . . McCarthy is a more appealing candidate personally . . . to the American people; [and] the Vice President has yet to project himself as a decisively positive presidential figure."

Then in Richmond, Virginia, the crowd was fantastic—more than Wallace or Nixon had drawn there, welcoming McCarthy with a three-minute ovation. But the man had very little to say to them. He was "not ready" to attack Humphrey. So he talked vaguely about "the power of reason and human judgment, the best instrument we have." The only person he criticized by name was John Bailey, the chairman of the Democratic Party. The audience left a little bewildered. I heard one couple saying, "Yeah, it was okay . . . but why didn't he tell us what to do?" And, "It was kind of vague, wasn't it?"

The next day there was a rapturous crowd at the airport in Raleigh. But McCarthy was brooding. His schedule was too long. He cut most of the meat from an anti-Humphrey text for the liberal Fulton County Democratic Club in Atlanta that night—and got another ecstatic reception.

On the courthouse steps in Lexington, Kentucky, he drew another strong crowd, and again at Vanderbilt University in Tennessee he was warmly received. His only bad stop was Louisville, where a fund-raising dinner drew practically no one. Speaking over the heads of the audience to reporters, the candidate who had constantly derided polls broke the scheduled release date on the latest Harris poll. It showed Humphrey ahead of Nixon just 37 to 35 percent, while McCarthy led 42 to 34. Rockefeller was leading Humphrey 37 to 34 percent, but McCarthy could beat Rocky 38 to 32. Harris was furious because his story was set for a Monday release, but McCarthy had succeeded in getting the results into the Sunday papers. In addition, we had discovered regional polls and private polls showing McCarthy leading Humphrey among Democratic voters in every large state, and two to one in California.

The message was clear. McCarthy was the only Democrat who could definitely beat the Republicans. It looked as though he could play it cool and wait for that lesson to sink in. But the polls shifted wildly in the next few weeks. Nixon shot up, McCarthy dropped, Rocky and Humphrey fluctuated, the pollsters explained and adjusted, and the polls meant nothing.

50 WHEN WE HIT ATLANTA I HAD A FREE HOUR BEFORE supper and decided to ease my tired mind in the hotel pool. While I swam, a young man, call him William, ran excitedly across the terrace. A sensitive boy from a distinguished family, William had been floundering at an Ivy League school until McCarthy came along and gave him a reason for living. He had got himself a job with the circus, leaping forward at every stop with microphone and portable recorder to preserve the candidate's every word. Now he had just heard the evening news. CBS had announced incorrectly that McCarthy was about to leave for Europe. William shouted the news to me; he was eager to be the first to sound the alarm. "So what?" I said from my swimming pool, and William treated my dullness to an elegant sneer. He had gone in a few months from sweetness and confusion to an imitated arrogance that might take its toll in the years to come. But I knew I had not helped him any by so quickly mocking his eagerness to serve.

I went to McCarthy's suite with the next day's text. He was eating dinner with his valet and two companions from the entourage. In the background Pinnochio played Vivaldi on a massive tape recorder: McCarthy ignored it.

The secretary came in with the next week's tentative schedule, which had been phoned in from Washington by our conscientious scheduler. The secretary scornfully read each item. "You don't want to do that, do you?" she said of a ghetto appearance. "No," McCarthy said, "tell that Norval

I'll do only one of those three. The weekend has to be open." They moved down the list, retaining only the least odious items. "Tell that Norval he won't be around here long!" (You may be sure she did.)

The conversation moved on to others who were running McCarthy for President. There was a pattern: twisted little descriptions of what people not there had done or said, offered up for a *coup de grâce* by the master. It was mentioned in passing that the CBS-TV man had tried to pull a fast one with the Europe announcement. Well, we knew all about him. It was nothing to get excited about.

"William was so excited," I heard myself saying, "that he nearly fell into the swimming pool."

I quickly excused myself and left. It was not the first time I had caught myself falling in with it. As long as I hoped for something from McCarthy, I was no more immune than the others.

51 LATE IN JULY I SNUCK OFF FOR A WEEKEND ON CAPE Cod, where I visited among liberals and intellectuals who had sent money to McCarthy, spoken and listened in his behalf at discotheques in Boston and New York. In the middle of writing their books and vacationing, they kept an anxious eye on yesterday's *New York Times*. Each afternoon on the beach they compulsively analyzed the country—and analyzed it all over again at the nightly cocktail party.

"How does he really feel about Negroes?" they wanted to know. "What's his program for the cities?" Even, "Is he a good person?" And a lot of questions beginning, "Why doesn't he . . ."

Yet a surprising number were true believers in McCarthy. For them that magic secret just had to be there. Each one believed himself specially tuned in to McCarthy's wisdom. The criticism others offered was so banal that it obviously did not apply. When McCarthy wouldn't work for political advantage, it was because of his principles; when he wouldn't fight for his principles, it was because of his "shrewd political instinct." Deep down, they were sure McCarthy knew what he was doing. Johnson had fallen, hadn't he? When the time came, McCarthy would make his move. There were things he knew. . . .

Then each one would take me aside and say, "He can't possibly make it, can he?"—with a tremulous little grin.

52 BACK IN WASHINGTON THERE WAS A NATIONAL STAFF engaged in talking on the phone all day—raising funds for themselves, fighting Finney, keeping in touch, and gathering information on delegates which no one used.

The financial operation was also in peculiar condition. Since McCarthy in this area, as in others, delegated full authority to no one, different fund-raisers kept different accounts—and kept hundreds of them, under hundreds of different committee titles, so that donors might give the legal maximum to each one. It got so that different factions of the campaign would go for funding to the fund-raiser who was sympathetic to them. This gave money-raisers a certain political power. Howard Stein, for instance, withheld a portion of the money he raised from the national organization, and used it to finance media projects of his own devising. As of the spring of 1969, the McCarthy finance committee did not know how much money Stein had in reserve or how much of it was left over after the campaign. Meanwhile Curt Gans raised money privately for his political operation, and money was raised privately by staff people in localities. There was no check on who was getting how much or what they were using it for. A donation to McCarthy, like political support of him, was purely a matter of faith. Some campaigners lived like kings while others dug into their own pockets and campaigned on their personal savings.

Goodwin returned in July, cheerful but more manic than before, as if constant action were the only remedy for the stunning loss he had suffered the second time over. Passing up speechwriting, he spent most of his time phoning and flying to see politicians, working up new statements for the press and trying to get McCarthy to do something effective on TV. Like Robert Kennedy, Goodwin relished continuous action, even if much of it turned out to be waste motion. He seemed always to have ten schemes, plans, plots and press releases going at the same time. But he worked well with McCarthy precisely because he did more than enough and left the candidate the role of passively going along or declining. When McCarthy did go along, he had a front man who would get the blame and whom he more than once made fun of to the press. But Goodwin was undaunted; he would wake up in the morning ready to wheel and deal, phone and fly. His way of getting McCarthy's okay was completely congenial to the candidate: he used shameless flattery. "Yes that's right, Senator, that's very interesting, that's funny, funny, that's very funny."

Meanwhile a team of writers in Washington was working on position papers, coordinating their efforts with the work of academic people in Cambridge and New York. McCarthy had announced he would be releasing two such papers every week, and they were necessary to counteract the impression that he lacked constructive ideas.

On July 10 we had an arms control paper from George Kistiakowsky and Jerome Wiesner, former scientific advisers for the Eisenhower and Kennedy Administrations, wherein McCarthy could urge important initiatives in disarmament. Also we had a paper on hunger in America, taken largely from *Hunger—USA* by the Citizens Board of Inquiry into Hunger and Malnutrition. If he approved it, McCarthy would have given some impact to the finding that in fiscal year 1968 the Department of Agriculture had not spent $527 million of the funds it had received to buy food for the hungry. But McCarthy was resting at a monastery in Collegeville, Minnesota, and it was impossible to reach him for approval. When we called the first night he couldn't be disturbed because he was watching the All-Star game on TV. The next day he was playing softball with the nuns.

Finally McCarthy did give his approval and the papers were released, but the Administrative Assistant came back from Minnesota and informed me that McCarthy was saying the hunger paper was wrong. Orville Freeman, the Secretary of Agriculture and a fellow Minnesotan, had called McCarthy and told him so. When I next saw McCarthy I asked him exactly where and how we had been in error, but he said no, no, it was okay. Still, hunger in America was not added to his public repertory.

Later on when people were beginning to press for formal statements of McCarthy's urban program, he took papers on jobs and housing off with him for a long weekend in Maine with Robert Lowell and the Secret Service. Unfortunately he didn't find time to read the papers over the weekend. He was finally prevailed upon to read and release them weeks later in the middle of August.

McCarthy had put himself in a leadership position, but he just wouldn't lead. It was not even possible to tell him this: he would shut off with the first few words. Or he would interrupt with a joke, a grin and a completely depersonalizing pat on the back. He had created a situation where his closest staff could not speak honestly. Of those around him on any regular basis who wanted McCarthy to act with more definite purpose, only Martin Peretz of Harvard told the candidate what he thought openly and without disguise. Peretz could get away with this partly because of his indispensable work on the finance committee, partly because he did not have to work with McCarthy from day to day.

The demoralization in Washington was summed up for me by a seminar I wandered into one night at our headquarters. A Frommian analyst had come down from New York to help the campaign, but of course there was no definite job to do. Yet the Frommian professed to find this refreshing and challenging. The candidate, in his wisdom, had granted the conditions for optimum creativity. The Frommian was worried about the negativity, the "anti-life" feeling, among so many of the young people who ran mimeo machines, licked envelopes and answered phones. He discovered his own role in convening a seminar to discuss the situation.

The discussion inevitably centered around the young workers' complaints that they had entered the campaign thinking they were involved in a crusade to reach and change America. Now they simply did not know what the hell was happening. There was no effort to do anything else but send around the candidate and make deals with politicians. They didn't mind much being cut off the payroll, but they saw McCarthy not coming through and they thought there was still a job to do.

The Frommian told them they were anti-life; McCarthy had given them freedom and they didn't know what to do with it. A young black man chimed in with a lecture on what it meant for him to "do his own thing." He used this concept to bully the whites about not having done more against racism. The Frommian agreed. "Your feeling towards the McCarthy campaign," he said, "depends on whether or not you can bear freedom." Clearly the kids could not bear it, not that way, and most of them now looked as if they thought it was all their own fault.

53 MEANWHILE THERE WERE STILL PEOPLE ALL AROUND the country yearning for McCarthy, painting signs, and arranging rallies. He was the only Democrat who could draw a crowd that summer. No one cared to see Humphrey—even when he walked through the Cleveland ghetto with Mayor Stokes.

On June 28, we got 50,000 people into Fenway Park in Boston—more than anyone ever drew there for anything. Credit for that record must go in part to Steven Cohen, a Harvard grad student who had worked full-time for McCarthy from the beginning, doing research or scheduling or anything that had to be done, and who now gave away two or three tickets for the same seats, so that thousands of ticket holders, even $100 ticket holders, were turned away when the crowd shot past capacity. Cohen had to get out of town fast—there were McCarthy people in Boston who wanted to throw him in jail.

The crowd was three-quarters students—healthy, well-fleshed, good-looking. The most desirable boys and girls in America, full of pure hate for their government.

The ball park sparkled green under the lights. Standing on the bandstand on second base, Lenny Bernstein cried, ". . . and coming now, from the centerfield bleachers, Gene McCarthy!" It would have been terrific then if McCarthy had ambled in alone (swinging two bats and throwing one away). Instead the metal door slid up and we saw the revolving red light of a cop car. A convoy of black limousines and police cars rolled slowly into left field. McCarthy walked to second base in a crowd of fifty cops and Secret Service men.

He looked strong and handsome up there on the bandstand with his chin held high. The steel eyes were bright blue in the arc light. I noticed on the infield that McCarthy's staff people chatted to one another throughout his speech. Somewhere along the line they had stopped listening. The fans in the stands roared at the familiar punch lines, but they too had stopped trying to follow the syntax. Our rallies had become rituals of the good and the pure. Our 50,000 beautiful people were showing something maybe about the future of American politics. But the grass-roots case for McCarthy was still open to question. You don't prove America is yours just by filling ball parks with college kids.

54 In July, in his Ft. Collins speech to the Colorado convention, McCarthy took exception to Humphrey's contention that incentives to private industry could solve the housing situation in the ghetto. The history of private industry was that it worked for its own profit and built very few low-rent units. Following our text he said he could not share the Vice President's pride in having "passed the liberal program." He then explained, in a pure improvisation, that liberals had passed only that part of the program which was "of benefit either to ourselves or to those who were . . . our relatives. . . . Medical care for the aged, for example . . . required . . . no great moral commitment, because there was always a selfish aspect." But the kind of programs needed now to deal with poverty and with the cities had to be understood "within the context of history" and required "deep moral commitment . . . because in many cases, people can see no benefit to themselves . . . but benefit only to other people." The programs would challenge us still further because they involved very large expenditures with no prospect of quick success, and demanded therefore real understanding and trust.

It was a fine performance intellectually, way beyond the scope of any other candidate. Yet on his way to Ft. Collins from the Denver airport, McCarthy had discovered that his caravan would stop to visit a community of Mexican workers striking a huge flower bulb farm. Their demands were basic —minimum wages and the right to organize. The caravan turned off the main highway and went down a long dusty side road. As the cars approached the outdoor meeting site, the road was lined with cheering farm workers. When McCarthy got out their band began to play and the workers shouted, "Viva McCarthy!" An organizer from Delano said, "This could really do it for us!" The reporters got out their pencils to take down McCarthy's endorsement.

"This is more like it!" Gorman said.

"Why do you get so over-excited?" remarked one of the traveling companions.

McCarthy stepped to the mike to give the workers his greeting—and that was all—there was no statement of support. He limply shook hands with a few of the leaders. Within minutes he was safely back in his car.

The people lining the road waved sadly as the line of new-rented cars passed by them once more and out of their lives forever. The organizers were angry. Said a depressed advance-man: "We're going to cause these people more grief and ourselves more hurt than if we never came."

The overview was fine—it was just reality that threw us.

55 ON AUGUST 13 MCCARTHY ARRIVED IN ST. LOUIS FOR his last campaign stop. McCarthy insurgents there had just pulled off a stunning upset in elections for the Democratic

county committee. But McCarthy was not heartened. He stood uneasily at a lectern set up in an airplane hangar, bent forward from the waist against the reporters and their lights, his left hand jammed deep as ever in his coat pocket, the right grabbing and clutching as he spoke for a hold on the edge of the wooden surface.

They asked how many ballots it would go in Chicago. Too tired then to keep up the pretense, he told them it would probably be over on the first ballot.

At Kiel Auditorium that night they had to turn away the crowds of students and suburban people. From out of nowhere McCarthy got his greatest ovation of the campaign: it would die and then swell again, going on for ten full minutes as the big man stood bent in his baggy suit in the middle of the stage. It must have been strange to find himself there, carried by one limited decision and an avalanche of uncontrollable forces. Yet he had done it and no one else, he was truly the one they applauded, the one man who had opened it up in 1968. He didn't know what to do about it: now and then he would lift his chin and raise his right hand in a restrained V-sign. And the people went on clapping, just as if he believed what they did, wanted what they wanted, as if he were in fact no more than their belief and their desire.

Watching closely I could see the blood come up once more. The adulation did something for him—he must have thought if anyone deserved it, it was he. But he of all people knew that no one deserved it, and if you tried to ride it, you'd be done for. You would stir them up, mislead them, mislead yourself. You'd be like all the rest, and the applause would be different.

There were some out there who were applauding because you were you, and you would stay who you were. But they could not know, no one would ever know. The more they applauded, the more alone he was. So he pushed out a soft underlip in a sign of firmness, raised two thick fingers in a qualified blessing, and he bore with it, He waited to be alone, his left hand hidden safe inside his pocket.

56 ON AUGUST 20, AS DEAN RUSK WAS LECTURING THE Democratic platform committee on the concept of "collective security," an aide came up and whispered in his ear. Russia had invaded Czechoslovakia, and Rusk scooped up his papers like an instructor who has concluded with a telling point.

That night Lyndon Johnson called a metting of the National Security Council. Already the politicians who had most piously defended our bombing and napalm in Vietnam rushed before the TV cameras to beat their breasts over Czechoslovakia and to cry up the need for ever more relentless hawkery.

Some of us were afraid that McCarthy would say nothing at all. I met him early the next morning with a statement that began, "This is a tragic day for freedom." It pointed out that Russia was imposing her own version of "collective security," that the invasion was "only the latest in a series of great power interventions that has gone on since the end of World War II." Probably there was little the U.S. could have done to stop it, but our position in Vietnam—including Johnson's reaffirmation of the bombing earlier that week—

"made it easier for the Russians to move as they did and . . . harder for us to mobilize world opinion against such acts."

When I walked into McCarthy's office, his first words to me were, "After all, Jeremy, it's not as if Hitler were marching in."

"I think it is," I said, "in some ways."

McCarthy then said the statement was okay; he would combine it with some notes of his own. He had a private call coming in, and I went to wait in the outer office.

Half an hour later the secretary emerged and handed me McCarthy's statement at the same time she gave a copy to Ken Reich of *The Los Angeles Times*, who was also in the office.

The statement began, "I do not see this as a major world crisis. It is likely to have more serious consequences for the Communist Party in Russia than in Czechoslovakia. I saw no need for a midnight meeting of the U.S. National Security Council." There followed a hasty adaptation of what I had written about our position in Vietnam and the need for new policies. I read it over slowly. There was not a single word condemning Russia.

I ran down the hall and grabbed Reich as he was about to get into the elevator, told him the statement had been released by mistake and was not official. He agreed to hold it for an hour while I tried to come up with another one. It was a large risk—I knew that if I couldn't change things in an hour, Reich would have an extra story about how a McCarthy aide had tried to suppress his candidate's statement. But if I couldn't change it, the effect would be disastrous anyway—especially with wavering delegates.

I started to run in to McCarthy, but the secretary cheerfully informed me that he could not be disturbed; he was being interviewed live over the phone by a small Midwestern radio network. Even if I broke in, he could not put down the receiver. For a second I thought of breaking in anyway, but I decided it would be more effective to call Goodwin.

Goodwin had just returned from Virginia, where he had been getting his hand in on Ted Kennedy's Vietnam speech, which would that afternoon mark Kennedy's re-entry into politics. I didn't have to waste any words with Goodwin, spelling out what was likely to happen with this Czech statement. Horrified, he tried to phone McCarthy right away, but naturally the secretary couldn't put him through. She was having a good morning.

Goodwin tried several times more with no success. Then he called and told me he had to let Ken Reich phone his story in. A reporter from *The New York Times* had seen Reich's copy and there would be no stopping it. I wished now I had broken in. I had spent fifteen minutes within five yards of McCarthy without being able to do a damn thing.

I sat down and looked at the statement and saw at once what had happened. McCarthy had been offended by Johnson's grandstand style. He had reacted to that rather than to the tanks rolling into Prague. That sort of thing had happened before and would happen again. Only a demagogue would claim virtue by denouncing evil. If people expected McCarthy to give the standard angry reaction, well they didn't understand what real style was. If they still needed at this point to test his values, let them think what they liked.

An elderly office aide moseyed by and cast further light by repeating what McCarthy had said that morning before I had arrived. When Hitler invaded, the aide said happily, Czechoslovakia was still a European country. But now it was an internal matter between two Communist states. Martin Peretz called on the phone from Chicago and was told that the intervention "was like sending federal troops to Detroit."

To hell with it then, I thought. At that moment I did not want McCarthy to be President. It was good the campaign was over. All that was left was Chicago, where at least I could work for the issues that mattered to me and the people who could keep faith with the cause.

Goodwin phoned me then to say he had finally gotten through and persuaded McCarthy to have a press conference that afternoon. He was cheerfully certain McCarthy would "straighten it all out." Why didn't I just come back?

We watched Ted Kennedy on TV come out in favor of an unconditional bombing halt, a significant decrease in the level of our military commitment, and a negotiated withdrawal of all foreign troops from South Vietnam. It was obvious that no one running for President would be able to support that war.

Then Goodwin went to bring McCarthy to the Statler-Hilton, where reporters were covering the platform hearings. It is amusing to think of their conversation in the car. Whatever Goodwin tried, it didn't work. McCarthy held tighter to his statement than Moses had held to the Ten Commandments. When they asked him what he would call a crisis, he answered, an invasion of France. When they asked him about the U.N. Security Council, he said it was all right with him if they wanted to play games with the U.N. He was right in his own terms, but he must have known that very few would understand. He was making absolutely clear what he had shown us in other ways from the beginning: that his style of presenting himself was more important than his campaign for President and all it stood for.

At last someone asked him outright why he showed no feeling for the Czechs or outrage against Russia.

"That goes without saying. Do I have to say it every time?"

"It's the compassion gap again," he said to one friendly reporter as he got into his limousine. He had reacted to that gap the same way Johnson had reacted to the credibility gap. And for the same reason.

57 THE NEXT DAY I WENT TO CHICAGO, WHERE IT WAS easy to see the negative effect of McCarthy's Czech statement—especially on delegates of east European backgrounds. Back East, Kenneth Galbraith finally persuaded McCarthy to release another statement. It began, ". . . I thought my position was clear. . . . Of course, I condemn this cruel and violent action. It should not really be necessary to say this. . . ."

The timing of that first Czech statement was particularly unfortunate in view of the fact that in Chicago, wherever there was alcohol and peanuts, Democrats were talking about whom they could get instead of Humphrey. Newsman with their expert inside count of a big majority solid for HHH suddenly discovered that the convention would begin with Daley holding out and Connally peeved.

Steven Mitchell could claim that it was our forcing Humphrey into line on the Unit Rule and on seating half the insurgents from Georgia that jeopardized Humphrey's already shaky southern support. Finney saw the southern recalcitrance as a sign that Johnson had not thrown his full weight behind Humphrey. And indeed, there was evidence that the Humphrey people feared Johnson was angling for a split convention and a triumphal re-entry.

Meanwhile everyone awaited the arrival of Ted Kennedy. It was now commonly accepted that no delegate count on earth would have stopped Ted's brother from taking the nomination. So maybe there was just barely a chance. . . . "Only God or Teddy can save us," moaned one California delegate. "Teddy *is* God!" he was answered by another.

The convention was still open—and frantic about it. It had been fixed for Humphrey. But it was not well fixed. The fixing was not what took it from McCarthy. If he had taken his movement to the different groups which the Democratic Party must represent—shown that he cared about them and wanted to work with them—added them to his strong suburban base—then he would truly have been a man of the people, and in all the weakness and clutching confusion of Chicago, the party would have had a hard time rejecting him.

58 MEANWHILE BACK IN WASHINGTON, HUMPHREY DUCKS out of a tentative preconvention TV debate with McCarthy, and McCarthy instructs Blair Clark not to press for a rescheduling. It is his movement that wants a showdown with Humphrey, not McCarthy. "I'm just as glad the debate's

off," he says. "Humphrey's getting to be such a bore I wouldn't want to spend half an hour with him."

59 DURING THE PLATFORM HEARINGS, GOODWIN AND HIS allies among the Kennedy people won a kind of triumph. They were able to write a minority plank on Vietnam which McCarthy, McGovern, and the Kennedy leadership could all agree on. It was a stiff plank based on Teddy's August 21 Vietnam speech—less precise than McCarthy in spelling out a coalition government, but still it would be utterly unacceptable to the Administration.

It was regrettable that McCarthy's own language could not have formed the basis of the peace plank. Partly he was too blunt for some politicians in accepting the implications of failure and defeat. Also McCarthy did not choose to involve himself in the hammering out of the plank. Necessarily, some sort of compromise was unavoidable, and given the circumstances, the plank was better than we could reasonably have hoped for.

When the minority committee first met, in fact, there was a danger that Ted Sorensen would take over the writing and pilot through a mild stop-the-bombing plank that Humphrey could magnanimously agree to run on.* Getting a single strong minority plank was an unexpected advantage. It meant that there could be a floor fight where doves could line up clearly against hawks. The issue of the war was going

*This effort was stopped, amusingly, by Goodwin's tipping off the press and creating a potentially embarrassing situation for his former speechwriting partner, who by then had political ambitions in New York State.

to be discussed in open debate before the American public, whether Johnson liked it or not.

The Sunday after the plank was agreed upon, we saw McCarthy on *Face the Nation* from Washington. It would have been a perfect time for him to start taking the debate to the public. He should have been well aware of the plank; Goodwin had cleared every change on the phone with him. To a large extent, this plank now represented the focus for the antiwar movement within the Democratic Party.

Yet when David Schoumacher pointed out the differences between the plank and McCarthy's campaign position, McCarthy could not find one good word for the plank. Calling it "their" plank, he could not respond to the simplest questions about it—as if he'd never heard of it. "That plank is not too important anyway," he said. "Well, I'm going out there today, David. We'll get it all straightened out, language and all."

He was then asked if Humphrey would be a good President. "I think he'd be a good President," McCarthy blandly said. "You can be a good President with bad policies."

60 On arrival in Chicago, McCarthy went straight to his room and stayed there for most of the convention. He posted his Senate office girls out in the corridor of the 23rd floor of the Conrad Hilton to ward off campaign staff. Within 24 hours he had heartened his supporters by telling interviewers from the Knight newspapers that the nomination was all over. When they heard this out at the convention,

Mitchell and Pat Lucey, McCarthy's floor manager, tried to phone McCarthy but could not get through to him. Shana Alexander reported approvingly in *Life* that McCarthy was spending a good deal of time tossing an orange around with his brother. His admirers formed a grandstand for the man who is not what anyone wants him to be. In exercising his utter independence McCarthy had locked himself into a kind of prison.

"Henceforth be masterless," quotes D. H. Lawrence as the American ideal. "Which is all very well," he says, "but it isn't freedom. . . . It is never really freedom till you find something you really *positively want to be*. And people in America have always been shouting about what they are *not*."

61 DESPITE THE PLEAS OF HIS POLITICALLY COMMITTED people, McCarthy refused to take the convention floor as the leader of his movement, arguing to the party and to the American people the case for a genuine peace plank, taking his fight on Vietnam as far as he could carry it. It is something every person who worked for him would have wanted him to do. And what did he have to lose?

Or he might have come before the convention on the rules fight, to tell them why citizens were trying to open up the Democratic Party in 1968, and to give them some vision of what the Democratic Party could be and how it could respond to the nation's needs. This would back up the work Stephen Mitchell had done on the various challenges, and identify McCarthy with the party's future. He could have told the country what a new politics in the Democratic Party could mean for America.

But it would have been bad form, for tradition has it that no candidate addresses the convention until nominees are chosen. McCarthy could not appear to be an opportunist, even if the opportunity was a chance to save his cause. He could not plead with the politicians and have them turn him down. He could not look like a loser, though he had scarcely tried to win.

The first time he had violated convention, there had been no question about winning or losing. He was challenging an incumbent President, and he would be canonized for his defense of virtue. That was all he had intended in the beginning, and now, in the end, that was what he was going to stick to. When Stephen Mitchell came to his suite to ask him one final time to take the floor as he had said he would, McCarthy told him, "I've always been running against Johnson. If Johnson goes, I'll go."

62

ON WEDNESDAY NIGHT I WENT ACROSS THE STREET and walked among the demonstrators in Grant Park. They were survivors of the battle in Lincoln Park, and they were bitter, but most of them seemed like gentle college kids come to town for a piece of history. The majority who hated the cops should not be confused with the minority who actively provoked them, or the smaller minority who attacked. According to the Walker Report, 5000 of the young people were from the Chicago area and 500 more came from out of town. Sam Brown estimated that 40 percent were "McCarthy kids" who had formerly worked as volunteers in one area or another. "The Mobilization" had fallen far short of its call for 100,000 revolutionary troops, and must have been worried at first about a public embarrassment.

I walked down the line where the cops stood holding their clubs and glaring into the park with incredible hostility. Occasionally someone would come up and taunt them as if the cops embodied all the forces above and beyond them. Huge TV floodlights bathed the park in an eerie dead white, like moonlight in the middle of the ocean. People moving cast deep shards of shadow through the crowd and into the dark trees. We were in an enchanted circle. If the moon went out, the shadows would engulf us, the wall of blue would break upon us, and we would drown in a sea of fury.

Most of the demonstrators sat on the ground talking and singing. Their favorite song was "We Shall Overcome." A few wore helmets and were dressed for battle—these were the ones who stood in line for the microphone and sent long harangues into the dark. A few kids lay stoned not five feet from the straining line of cops. Here and there a couple of young black men or lower-class hoods stood on the margins of the light in a kind of hostile sympathy.

Suddenly someone called me. Two former students of mine, sweeter girls you could not find. A year ago they had no interest in politics whatsoever. I met some grad students who'd driven down from Madison, sensible people who hate the war but also hate to get hurt. A Chicago housewife I'd known in college. Finally a youngster from New York, stretched out happily on the grass. "Hey, man! I've been talking to delegates!" Turns out he really has, he met them in the park. And that's why he came to Chicago: to talk to delegates and convince them to vote for McCarthy. At three in the morning, there must be fifty delegates sitting with the kids in Grant Park. From time to time a chant goes up to the people in the Hilton: "We want Gene! Dump the Hump!"

From what I saw, most of the kids who came to Chicago wanted change, but were not dedicated revolutionaries. They wanted the system to start working, and many of them believed that the Chicago convention was its last chance. They thought if the Democratic Party wouldn't represent those who were against the war and in favor of a new kind of racial and economic justice in America, then a revolution might be inevitable. But they thought that the revolution would be made by forces far larger than themselves. Some of them thought that violence in the end might be the only way, but only a very few of them were personally violent. They identified with the victims of violence—which turned out to be not so unreasonable.

THINK OF YOUR DESIRES AS REALITY says a slogan in one of the underground papers they distributed that week. A childish indulgence on first reading. But wasn't that what we all were doing during 1968? And what could we have done without it?

63 ON THURSDAY THE KIDS WERE BENT ON COMMITTING the terrible crime of marching without a permit. Some of them took a hill in the park and planted a Vietcong flag there, so naturally the brave policemen had to chase them

and gas them. Looking out a window of the Hilton I saw white puffs of gas far up Michigan Avenue. In five minutes we were crying up on the 23rd floor.

A call came from the Amphitheater: Julian Bond would second McCarthy's nomination in an hour, but he didn't have a speech. A speech was quickly written. It ended: "When others held back, Gene McCarthy assumed that the American people could bear the truth—and we learned that not only could they bear it—they were hungry for truth, starving for frankness and honesty—and hoping and praying for a candidate who would speak freely and openly. . . .

"Fellow delegates, the people of America are watching us now—as indeed the whole world is watching us. They are looking to the Democratic Party to honor their faith in democracy. . . . It is not too late. . . ." etc.

Of course it was too late, or it would have been harder to write the speech.

64 It was too late also for me to risk a drive to the Amphitheater; the hotel was surrounded by surging crowds and cops. We had to get the speech on the teletype, but the machine kept breaking down. While I waited I looked out the window from the 15th floor. Gorgeous afternoon, the lake a flawless blue. But tear gas still hung in the air, and up Michigan Avenue the street suddenly filled with people coming our way.

The cops set up a line at the intersection and blockaded them away from the Hilton. I saw the Poor People's mule train being drawn through the line, past the Hilton and around the corner, and I caught my breath. Sure enough, they weren't going to permit the crime of blocking traffic. The line of cops moved forward to clear the street. Here and there an individual resisted, or stumbled—and in an instant the cops were lunging forward and clubbing heads with all their might. You could hear the sodden *thuck* of club on skull clear up to the 15th floor.

It was worse than anything I later saw on television. Cops chased kids off into the park and out of sight among the trees, emerged with one cop dragging a boy or girl by the leg and another cop running alongside clubbing in the groin. A man tried to carry a bleeding woman into the hotel and they were both clubbed and thrown into the wagon. People ran up to plead with cops beating kids on the ground and the cops turned around and clubbed them. They clubbed men in white who knelt to carry off the fallen and clubbed anyone with a camera on his neck. They charged people on the sidewalk and smashed them up against the building as we heard terrible screams. Very few were fighting back; I saw none with weapons. What I saw was blue helmets surging forward in waves, clubbing and clubbing and clubbing.

All at once I was angrier than I would ever have believed. Down in the street I saw what we'd been waiting for all summer. The same violence that burnt villages, the violence that smashed up anything it couldn't understand. I was raging with the force of everything I'd held down day by day working against my pride for the sake of some damn imaginary cause which was a losing cause anyway. Which could be wiped out at any moment by blue helmets who took the right to club.

The blues were clustered now straight underneath the

window. I reached for a heavy lamp—and some teen-age girls rushed to stop me. "You'll be as bad as they are!"

"You're right," I said. I pulled back from the window. But I knew if I'd had a machine gun then I'd have mowed them down.

Later, when that knowledge sunk in, I was sick and scared of more than just the cops.

65 LATER THAT NIGHT GOODWIN, GORMAN AND I SNUCK out through the hotel basement and rode to the stockyards in a Secret Service limousine which Goodwin commandeered. In a little room at the Amphitheater, Steve Mitchell, Pat Lucey, and the McCarthy floor managers were gathered. A call came through for Goodwin: McCarthy wanted to withdraw his name before the balloting. Goodwin unhesitatingly started to type up a statement. "But why?" I said. "Why?"

McCarthy said later it might have "stabilized" the situation. "This isn't my party," he had said. "This isn't the Democratic Party." Maybe he wanted to show that, to show them they had to pay the price. But I didn't like it. It was the ultimate withdrawal. It implied an excuse we hadn't earned.

Harold Hughes of Iowa was on the phone with McCarthy. Gravely he was telling McCarthy that he owed it to his supporters to stay in. The managers were clustered around Hughes, waiting. He looked around questioningly: opinion was about evenly divided. Hughes repeated what he'd said before.

I never knew what McCarthy said, but his name was not

withdrawn. It was too late anyway; the balloting had begun. When Humphrey went over the top, I was out on the convention floor, slipping among Daley's goons to help get word to the peace people of a meeting afterwards.

About three hundred delegates jammed into a caucus room later and told each other it was only the beginning. For the first time, there was no mention of McCarthy's name.

I guess there were about five hundred of us by the time we walked down Michigan Avenue with candles. In Grant Park the delegates were warmly greeted by the demonstrators. They sat down together and sang freedom songs by candlelight. The stars were out: it was a little like campers and counselors. Sweet.

Goodwin got on their PA and spoke to the young people. "We want to control our own lives," he said. "That's what you're all about. And we'll live to see the day!"

Goodwin didn't know then that Richard Nixon would say those same things throughout his campaign. The kids didn't know either. They responded with one last round of We Want Gene! and Dump the Hump!

66 The next morning McCarthy made a farewell speech to staff, delegates, and volunteers. He was in a great mood—like a man let out of jail. When they stood up and cheered he said, "If you keep on this way, I may lose my cool. I may not show active compassion, but I may show a kind of particular joy." The applause did continue, but I could not tell if McCarthy fulfilled his end of the bargain.

Calling them the government-in-exile, he counted up for them how they'd succeeded in terms of raising the issues they had set out to raise, how the nation and the party, thanks to them, would never be the same. "If you purify the pond," he said, "some of the water lilies die." He called for "one-man, one-vote" at the next Democratic Convention.

A voice called, "Forget the convention!"

"We've forgotten the convention," McCarthy said: "We're beyond it!" And they applauded.

"We've forgotten the Vice President!"

"We've forgotten the platform!"

"And," he climaxed, "we've forgotten the Chairman of the National Committee!"

He wound up telling us that "We were willing to open the box and see what America was. We had that kind of trust and that kind of confidence. And when we opened it, we found"—*what? what?*—"that the people of this nation were not wanting."

Is that what we found?

67 I WAS GIVEN A LIFT TO THE AIRPORT BY BOB SCHEER. I was so tired and depressed I couldn't talk straight, but Scheer was elated. "This has been a good thing for us," he gloated. "Thousands of kids have been radicalized by what happened here."

I wasn't sure. I remembered the kids in the park chanting for Gene even after the clubbings and the nomination. But Scheer had ten examples for every one of mine—and sure enough the newspapers and magazines soon backed him up. Youth now reads that it was "radicalized" at Chicago, and may even be ready to buy that image.

But I still don't know what that word means in terms of politics. McCarthy's student volunteers were already radical in wanting to change the American political structure rather than slowly reform it, radical in wanting to redistribute power. But in context, "radicalization" seemed to mean the abandonment of politics in favor of violence. Scheer had with him a gleeful SDS kid who was predicting that he and his would break up everything in sight. Like the cops I talked to, he was still high from the violence.

Since Chicago I've found that most student activists no longer feel they can make an absolute argument against the use of force. They talk sometimes as if democratic methods are washed up in this country. But I know too that if a liberal Democrat against the war—even one of the regular party men like George McGovern or Ted Kennedy or Harold Hughes—took the initiative in leading a campaign to turn this country around, most of the students would work for him. There would be a tendency for an autonomous student movement to develop around such a campaign, and it would probably push toward goals beyond the scope of its candidate.

The problem is not the students—an overwhelming majority of them are ready to work for the ideals they were taught in their high school civics classes. The problem is the rest of the country, and by the middle of 1969 Richard Nixon was betting they weren't ready.

NOBODY KNOWS

68 Some last questions. Was the McCarthy campaign a fluke of peculiar circumstance, or a forerunner of a really new kind of politics?

It is hard to believe that 1968 will mark the end of the kinds of energy and sentiment that went into the effort to force a peace candidate on the Democratic Party, even if the war in Vietnam were an accident and were to end tomorrow. For beyond the particulars of the war is the basic issue of power: who in our society makes the decision to go to war? Who runs the cities in which we live so badly, so helplessly? What we saw in the outpouring of volunteers for McCarthy is the emergence of a new class—a class of educated professionals and students who are not connected to bread-and-butter politics and who are under-represented in the Democratic and Republican parties. Their concerns and their values simply are not reflected in a governmental-congressional setup which is based on achieving a balance of cash interests. The new class takes its affluence and education for granted; it can't be bought off or balanced off. It wants to feel that enlightened individuals can exercise a decent control over the circumstances of their lives—from the wars they fight to the air they breathe. It wants to be part of the process of government. And it is learning that it cannot be unless the process is changed.

That was one of the lessons of 1968: that there are certain institutions in our society which are undemocratic agglomerations of power; that they defy public control or participation;

that in critical cases they exercise a decisive effect on the President, the Congress, and the two major parties. I refer chiefly to the military and the corporate structure. The independent power they exercise is blatantly incompatible with the distribution of power among equal citizens. 1968 was the first time this conflict was dramatized, however imperfectly, in a national campaign. As a result of this campaign, however, there were no institutional changes. No line of power opened up—so it is inevitable that the conflict will resume.

When it does, the new class will be anxious to find allies among marginal groups which also desire power and participation. McCarthy-style snobbery is an anachronism of diminishing political value. The new kinds of self-consciousness among black people and working class people will demand new definitions of common interest among all groups who are exploited, discontent and powerless. In fact, the success of the new class in opening up the political process may be the only alternative to the cycle of racial violence and repression. For it should be apparent by now that black Americans will not be assimilated by anything short of structural institutional change—by a Congress, for example, which in its procedures and operations places public over private interest.

At the moment the forces for a democratic transformation of this country are in disarray. Perhaps their emergence in 1968 was premature, no matter how urgently needed or desired. For the new politics is built on air. It has no structural base, and few programs or operations that maintain strength and discipline between national elections. The new politics is at present much too dependent on charismatic leaders—and wastes its energies in arguments over who is really our hero and whose followers can be accepted into the club. It will not realize its potential until organizations can be built which are larger than any candidate. Only when the new politics creates a political structure and gets it working, will it have candidates who more clearly conform to its ideals.

It is hard to imagine the new politics getting started without some dramatic candidate like McCarthy who half sees and half turns away. Still, it was unnecessary for so many of McCarthy's supporters to repeat the old American tradition of idealizing a politician as a leader beyond politics. The tradition has its virtues. It enables candidates to shake free of narrow partisan or ideological concerns. It permits a wider criticism of the past, as with McCarthy. But it also is vulnerable to a sentimental ineffectuality: as with all the Republican liberals who never quite know what they are doing or manage really to put up a whole-hearted fight for their party's nomination. When the hero is beyond politics, there is a built-in tendency to political collapse—or to a victory that changes nothing.

One might conclude from 1968 that we are at a moment in American life when it may be possible to organize around issues. Certain problems are so readily connected that to discover one is soon to discover all. The way we have sunk deeper in Vietnam and our justifications for it point to the operations and influence of the military. This raises the question of democratic participation and control. It is obvious, then, that Congress fails to represent the public in critical ways. Can such a Congress set the priorities necessary to relieve the racial crisis and rebuild our cities? Clearly it is unduly responsive to the pressures of corporations—which also affect foreign policy and work in cooperation with the military. I am describing not a conspiracy, but a set of interlocking institutions which betray the democratic intent of our society and which are inadequate to deal with the crisis at hand.

Given the interlocking, it is clear that the forces of change can get at the military and the corporations through Congress. A coordinating organization might facilitate new politics grass-roots efforts in hundreds of campaigns across the country. Nominations procedures could also be affected. Candidates could be pledged in advance to a new kind of Congress—and could be given expert help in explaining why to the electorate.

This sort of organization could have an effect on both political parties, or lead to a new party of its own. Its basic electoral orientation need not exclude tie-ups with other sorts of action designed to bring direct pressure on the military and on the corporations. Protests, boycotts, strikes and various forms of community action are quite compatible with electoral campaigns; the same indivdiuals could be involved in both. And clearly programs are needed which bring students and black people in contact with the white working class, and which show them that in terms of the larger issues they have interests in common.

On the other hand, it could well be that the contradictions are too severe, the cleavages too vast, the resistance too absolute—and we are in for an increasingly violent exchange between far left and far right which will pre-empt the possibility of meaningful change. In that event, the McCarthy campaign will be cited not as a surprising beginning, but as a last lost chance.

Yet as long as we believe we have some choice in the

matter, it will be worthwhile to look back upon the McCarthy campaign and the curious figure at its center. In trying to learn the lessons that might bring success where he had to settle for an exalted failure, we could do no better, I think, than to grant him his request for "a rather harsh and difficult moral judgment upon our own course of conduct"—though by "our own course" he did not, of course, mean his course.

The McCarthy campaign, in all its vicissitudes and contradictions, told us something we had not known about ourselves and our country. If we can see it as it was, there is hope yet we will make something better.